JAMES

A BEGINNING-INTERMEDIATE GREEK READER

JAMES

A Beginning-Intermediate Greek Reader

Darian Lockett ◆ Wes Lynd

GlossaHouse
Wilmore, KY
www.glossahouse.com

James: A Beginning-Intermediate Greek Reader

GlossaHouse, LLC
110 Callis Circle
Wilmore, KY 40390

James: A Beginning-Intermediate Greek Reader / edited by Darian Lockett and Wes Lynd

xvi, 119pp. 22 cm. — (AGROS Series)

Includes bibliographical references.

ISBN-13: 9781942697879

ISBN-10: 1942697872

Library of Congress Control Number: 2019950255

The fonts used to create this work are available from www.linguistsoftware.com/lgku.htm.

Babel Lexicography (BabLex), licensed by J. Klay Harrison and Chad M. Foster, 2012.

Koine Greek Paradigm Chart created by J. Klay Harrison in consultation with Fredrick J. Long.

Cover Design by Asa Harrison

Cover Created by T. Michael W. Halcomb

Book Design by Chad M. Foster and J. Klay Harrison

Typesetting by Fredrick J. Long

This Series is dedicated to all who have struggled to make Greek a regular part of their study of Scripture.

Contents

AGROS

Accessible Greek Resources and Online Studies

SERIES EDITORS

T. Michael W. Halcomb   Fredrick J. Long

AGROS

The Greek word ἀγρός is a field where seeds are planted and growth occurs. It can also denote a small village or community that forms around such a field. The type of community envisioned here is one that attends to Holy Scripture, particularly one that encourages the use of biblical Greek. Accessible Greek Resources and Online Studies (AGROS) is a tiered curriculum suite featuring innovative readers, grammars, specialized studies, and other exegetical resources to encourage and foster the exegetical use of biblical Greek. The goal of AGROS is to facilitate the creation and publication of innovative and inexpensive print and digital resources for the exposition of Scripture within the context of the global church. The AGROS curriculum includes five tiers, and each tier is indicated on the book's cover: Tier 1 (Beginning I), Tier 2 (Beginning II), Tier 3 (Intermediate I), Tier 4 (Intermediate II), and Tier 5 (Advanced). There are also two resource tracks: Conversational and Translational. Both involve intensive study of morphology, grammar, syntax, and discourse features. The conversational track specifically values the spoken word, and the enhanced learning associated with speaking a language in actual conversation. The translational track values the written word, and encourages analytical study to aide in understanding and translating biblical Greek and other Greek literature. The two resource tracks complement one another and can be pursued independently or together.

Abbreviations

1st	first person
2nd	second person
3rd	third person
Ϝ, ϝ	digamma (Greek letter used up to about 200 BC)
abl.	ablative
abs.	absolute, absolutely
acc.	accusative
act.	active
add.	additional, additionally
adj.	adjective
adv.	adverb, adverbial, adverbially
alt.	alternately
ans.	answer
ante.	antecedent
aor.	aorist
app.	apposition, appositional
art.	article
attrib.	attributive, attributively
aug.	augment
Barclay	Newman, Barclay M., ed. *A Concise Greek-English Dictionary of the New Testament.* Stuttgart: Deutsche Bibelgesellschaft, 1993.
BDAG	Bauer, F., F. W. Danker, et al., eds. *A Greek-English Lexicon of the New Testament and Other Early Christian Literature*. 3rd ed. Chicago: University of Chicago Press, 2000.
beg.	beginning
btw.	between
cmpd.	compound
comp.	comparative, comparatively
conj.	conjunction
constr.	construct, construction.
correl.	correlative
corresp.	corresponding, correspondingly

dat.	dative
dem.	demonstrative
dep.	deponent
diph.	diphtong
dir.	direct
dissim.	dissimilate, dissimilation
ditrans.	ditransitive (trivalent)
ECM	Aland, Barbara, Kurt Aland, Gerd Mink and Klaus Wachtel, eds. *Novum Testamentum Graecum: Editio Critica Maior*, vol. 4: *Catholic Letters*. 4 installments. Stuttgart: Deutsche Biblegesellschaft, 1997–2005.
e.g.	exempli gratia, Latin: "for example"
em.	emendation
emph.	emphatic
encl.	enclitic
equiv.	equivalent
esp.	especially
euphem.	euphemism
fem.	feminine
fig.	figurative, figuratively
fut.	future
gen.	genitive, genitival
GNT	Greek New Testament
Greeven	Huck, Albert. *Synopse der drei ersten Evangelien/ Synopsis of the First Three Gospels*. 13th ed. Revised by Heinrich Greeven. Tübingen: Mohr Siebeck, 1981.
hist.	historical
Holmes	Michael W. Holmes
imper.	impersonal (avalent)
impf.	imperfect
impv.	imperative
indef.	indefinite
indic.	indicative
indir.	indirect

inf.	infinitive
init.	initial
instr.	instrumental
inter.	interrogative
intrans.	intransitive (monovalent)
irreg.	irregular
L&N	Louw, Johannes P., and Eugene A. Nida, eds. *Greek-English Lexicon of the New Testament: Based on Semantic Domains*. 2 vols. 2nd ed. New York: United Bible Societies, 1989.
length.	lengthen, lengthened
lit.	literally
loc.	locative
LSJ	Liddell, Henry G., R. Scott, H. S. Jones, and R. McKenzie, eds. *A Greek-English Lexicon*. Rev. 9th ed. Oxford: Clarendon, 1996.
masc.	masculine
mid.	middle
metaph.	metaphor, metaphorical
MH	morphology help
Mounce	Mounce, William D. *The Morphology of Biblical Greek*. Grand Rapids: Zondervan, 1994.
Muraoka	Muraoka, T. *A Greek-English Lexicon of the Septuagint*. Louvain: Peeters, 2009.
neg.	negative, negate(d)
neut.	neuter
nom.	nominative, nominal
NA	Greek text of the NA^{27} and UBS^{4}
NA^{27}	Aland, Barbara, K. Aland, J. Karavidopoulos, C. M. Martini, and B. M. Metzger, eds. *Novum Testamentum Graece*. 27th ed. Stuttgart: Deutsche Bibelgesellschaft, 1993.
NA^{28}	Aland, Barbara, K. Aland, J. Karavidopoulos, C. M. Martini, B. M. Metzger, and Institute for New Testament Textual Research, eds. *Novum Testamentum Graece*, 28th ed. Stuttgart: Deutsche Bibelgesellschaft, 2012.

NIV	Goodrich , Richard J., and Albert L. Lukaszewski, eds., *A Reader's Greek New Testament*. Grand Rapids: Zondervan, 2003.
NRSV	New Revised Standard Version
obj.	object
opt.	optative
paren.	parenthetical
pass.	passive
per.	person, personal
periphr.	periphrastic
pf.	perfect, perfective
pl.	plural
plpf.	pluperfect
PN	personal name
pos.	positive
poss.	possessive
post.	postcedent
prec.	preceding
pred.	predicate
pref.	prefix, prefixed
prep.	preposition, prepositional
pres.	present
pron.	pronoun
prtc.	participle
reduc.	reduction
redupl.	reduplicate, reduplication
ref.	reference
reflex.	reflexive
rel.	relative
RP	Robinson, Maurice A., and William G. Pierpont, eds. *The New Testament in the Original Greek: Byzantine Textform 2005*. Southborough, Mass.: Chilton, 2005.
SBL	Society of Biblical Literature
SBLGNT	Holmes, Michael W. *The Greek New Testament: SBL Edition*. Atlanta: Society of Biblical Literature, 2010. http://sblgnt.com/.

SBLGNT[app]	Apparatus of SBLGNT
sg.	singular
Smyth	Smyth, Herbert Weir. *Greek Grammar*. Revised by Gordon M. Messing. Cambridge, Mass.: Harvard University Press, 1984.
subj.	subjunctive
subst.	substantival, substantive
suf.	suffix, suffixed
superl.	superlative
suppl.	suppletive
syn.	synonym
TDNT	Friedrich, Gerhard, and Gerhard Kittel, eds. *Theological Dictionary of the New Testament*. 10 vols., tr. by G. W. Bromiley. Grand Rapids, Mich.: Eerdmans, 1964–76.
TH	Translation Help
TLNT	Spicq, Ceslas. *Theological Lexicon of the New Testament*. 3 vols. Peabody, Mass.: Hendrickson, 1994.
TR	Textus Receptus ("Received Text")
trans.	transitive (divalent)
translit.	transliteration (of a loan word into Greek)
Treg	Tregelles, Samuel Prideaux. *The Greek New Testament, Edited from Ancient Authorities, with their Various Readings in Full, and the Latin Version of Jerome*. London: Bagster; Stewart, 1857–1879.
Treg[marg]	margin of Treg
Trenchard	Trenchard, Warren C. *Complete Vocabulary Guide to the Greek New Testament*. Rev. ed. Grand Rapids, Mich.: Zondervan, 1998.
UBS[4]	Aland, B., K. Aland, J. Karavidopoulos, C. M. Martini, and B. M. Metzger, eds. *The Greek New Testament*. 4th rev. ed. New York: United Bible Societies, 2006.
voc.	vocative

WH	Hort, Fenton John Anthony, and Brooke Foss Westcott. *The New Testament in the Original Greek.* 2 vols. Cambridge: Macmillan, 1881.
WH^{app}	*Appendix* (vol. 2 of WH)
WH^{marg}	margin of WH
Works (TJ)	Jackson, Thomas, ed. *The Works of the Rev. John Wesley, M.A.* 14 vols. Grand Rapids: Baker, 1978.

Preface to the Readers

And men who speak the Latin tongue, of whom are those I have undertaken to instruct, need two other languages for the knowledge of Scripture, Hebrew and Greek, that they may have recourse to the original texts if the endless diversity of the Latin translators throw them into doubt.

— Saint Augustine, *De Doctrina Christiana* 2.11.16

Do I understand Greek and Hebrew? Otherwise, how can I undertake, (as every Minister does,) not only to explain books which are written therein, but to defend them against all opponents? Am I not at the mercy of everyone who does understand, or even pretends to understand, the original? For which way can I confute his pretense? Do I understand the language of the Old Testament? critically? at all? Can I read into English one of David's Psalms, or even the first chapter of Genesis? Do I understand the language of the New Testament? Am I a critical master of it? Have I enough of it even to read into English the first chapter of St. Luke? If not, how many years did I spend at school? How many at the University? And what was I doing all those years? Ought not shame to cover my face?

— John Wesley, "An Address to the Clergy," *Works* (TJ) X:491.

Learning Koinē Greek can be a daunting task. Some students learn just enough to fulfill degree requirements and then forget most of what they learned. This is a sad fact, especially since many people would love such an opportunity to read Scripture in the original languages. Forgetting Greek may not be intentional, yet it is a reality for numerous students. While many resources are available that teach the grammatical basics of Koinē Greek, the beginning student is often still not able to read their Greek New Testament (NT). Beginning students are often hindered from reading the Greek NT due to a lack of vocabulary or unfamiliarity with Koinē Greek syntax and idioms.

The *Beginning-Intermediate Greek Readers* of the New Testament are Tier 3 resources that assume the completion of beginning Greek instruction. They are designed to build confidence and encourage the reading of the Greek NT by providing vocabulary glosses, morphological explanations, and translation helps, while also assisting the student to transition from beginning into intermediate Greek studies. By carefully working through these *Beginning-Intermediate Greek Readers*, students will find value interacting with the Greek NT and see how grammatical classifications affect meaning and translation in context.

Any student who uses these *Beginning-Intermediate Greek Readers*, will be able to apply her/his beginning Greek education and read directly from the Greek NT. By doing so, it is hoped that the Greek NT might become a part of daily reading and proclamation. Interpreters, pastors, and students will find the *Beginning-Intermediate Greek Readers* beneficial for careful investigation of the Greek NT.

J. Klay Harrison
May 2013

How to Use the Readers

The *Beginning-Intermediate Greek Readers* of the NT are designed to be user-friendly guides for reading the Greek NT. These resources will provide footnotes with morphological and textual helps, variants between *The Greek New Testament: SBL Edition* and the standard critical editions of the Greek NT, and all vocabulary that occurs 49 times or less. Additionally, each chapter is introduced with a vocabulary list of these infrequent words that occur within the chapter. The list is sorted by word frequency as found in the chapter, arranged from most to least frequent.

The Greek Text

The main Greek text is *The Greek New Testament: SBL Edition* (SBLGNT). This edition is a critical text of the GNT and includes a text-critical apparatus. The SBLGNT text and apparatus are explained in the "Introduction to the SBLGNT," which follows this section. The "Introduction to the SBLGNT" expounds not only how the SBLGNT text was assembled but also how to use the text-critical apparatus found in Appendix I. The introduction was written by Michael Holmes and is also found in *The Greek New Testament: SBL Edition*.

> SBLGNT is the *The Greek New Testament: SBL Edition*. Copyright 2010 Society of Biblical Literature and Logos Bible Software [ISBN 978-1-58983-535-1]. The SBLGNT text can be found online at http://sblgnt.com. Information about the "Society of Biblical Literature" can be found at http://sbl-site.org and "Logos Bible Software" at http://logos.com.

The Text-Critical Apparatus

The text-critical markings found in the SBLGNT point the reader to the apparatus, which is included in Appendix I of each *Beginning-Intermediate Greek Reader*. For an explanation of the text critical marks and the apparatus, please see "Introduction to the SBLGNT."

The Footnotes

For ease of reading, the *Beginning-Intermediate Greek Readers* use footnotes as a guide. The footnotes provide four categories of information; 1) lexical aid, 2) morphology help (MH), 3) translation help (TH), and 4) NA (NA^{27}/UBS^{4}) and NA^{28} variants. Each category is described below.

1. If a Greek word occurs 49 times or less in the SBLGNT, then lexical aid is provided in a footnote. Each Greek word is provided in lexical (dictionary) form. Thus, all verbs are presented in **pres. act. indic. 1st sg**. conjugation. Pronouns and adjectives are shown in **nom. sg. masc.** form followed by the **nom. sg. fem.** and **nom. sg. neut.** endings. The lexical form for a noun is the **nom. sg.** full inflection followed by the **gen. sg.** ending and then the respective article, which indicates gender. After the word's lexical form, glosses are found in italics. These glosses are general meanings for the Greek word, so they are not comprehensive of the word's complete lexical range. Since words only have meaning in context, there are times when a standard gloss is not appropriate for adequate translation. In these instances, a contextual gloss will be suggested in a bold italic font following a semicolon, e.g.,

1 λόγος, ου, ὁ, *word, speech, matter;* ***concept***.

In this example, the Greek word in question is a form of λόγος. Since λόγος is a noun, the fully inflected nom. sg. masc. form (λόγος) is provided. Then follows the gen. ending (ου), which lets the reader know this is a 2nd declension noun. The article (ὁ) is given in nom. sg. masc. inflected form. Since ὁ is masc., the article then indicates λόγος is a masc. noun. Thus, the entire lexical form is λόγος, ου, ὁ. Then, to translate λόγος, the entry suggests using one of the following standard glosses: *word, speech, matter*. However, it appears these standard glosses do not capture the true meaning of λόγος within the given context. So, the entry also provides a contextual gloss to better fit this particular context. Thus, here it is suggested that λόγος should be translated as ***concept***.

2. Morphology Help (MH) is also provided in the footnotes. These notes supply potentially difficult parsing, explain word formation, and clarify any morphological issues, e.g.,

> 2 MH: fut. act. indic. 2nd pl. from μένω = μεν (root) + εσ (tense formative) + ετε (thematic 2nd pl. ending) › μεν + εετε (σ btw. two vowels elides) › μενεῖτε (vowels contract; ε + ε = εῖ).

The initials MH in this footnote denotes the following as morphology help. The particular word in question is μενεῖτε. The parsing is given along with the lexical form. Then a detailed explanation shows step by step how the inflected verb was formed.

3. The third footnote category is the Translation Help (TH), which provides brief explanations for difficult grammar, idioms, morphology, and syntax, e.g.,

> 3 TH: λόγου is dir.obj. of ἀκούει.

The initials TH in the footnote illustration marks what follows as a translation help. λόγου is the word in question within the main Greek text. The TH is telling the reader that, in this clause, λόγου is functioning as the direct object of the verb ἀκούει.

Students should be aware that at times certain phrases will be placed in front of the verb for various reasons. Though it is beyond the purpose of the *Beginning-Intermediate Greek Readers* to discuss prominence and emphasis, there will be some Translation Helps (TH) marking the Greek wordage as "fronted."

4. Any difference in spelling between the SBLGNT, NA, and NA[28] are also available in a footnote. This will be evidenced by "NA has" (or "NA[28] has") and then the textual difference. Although some of these variants are presented in the text-critical apparatus found in the Appendix I, they are included in the footnotes for sake of quick reference, e.g.,

4 NA has ῥῆμα.

Here the footnote informs the reader that the NA Greek texts have ῥῆμα where the SBLGNT has something different.

The Vocabulary and Glosses

The beginning Koinē Greek student should learn every word that occurs in the GNT 50 times or more (310 words). Glosses for these high frequency words appear in Appendices II and III. They are listed both by frequency (for vocabulary retention) and in alphabetical order (for quick reference). Every word that occurs 49 times or less in the SBLGNT will be glossed in the footnote section. Additionally, each chapter is introduced with a vocabulary list of these glossed words that occur within the chapter. The list is sorted by word frequency as found in the chapter, arranged from most to least frequent in the SBLGNT. All word frequencies are based upon lexical occurrences in the SBLGNT, not the NA or NA[28].

The goal in establishing vocabulary glosses is to provide accurate yet concise glosses for every word. Knowing that words only have meaning in context, standard glosses will not suffice for every word occurrence. Such is the limit of a gloss. Whenever a standard glosses does not fix the context, a contextual gloss will be available in a footnote.

All glosses are a collaborative effort between the author(s), AGROS Editorial Board, and Babel Lexicography (BabLex). These glosses are the result of independent research and the consultation of numerous resources, which include but are not limited to: Barclay, BDAG, Muraoka, LSJ, L&N, TDNT, TLNT, and Trenchard.

The Appendices

The appendices of the *Beginning-Intermediate Greek Readers* include four sections: Appendix I: SBLGNT Apparatus, Appendix II: Vocabulary 50 times or more sorted by frequency, Appendix III: Vocabulary 50 times or more arranged alphabetically, and Appendix IV: Koinē Greek Paradigm Charts. Each appendix is described below.

Appendix I: SBLGNT Apparatus. Throughout the Greek text, text-critical marks will point the reader to the SBLGNT Apparatus (SBLGNT^{app}). This apparatus has been placed in Appendix I. For an explanation of the text-critical marks and how to use the SBLGNT^{app}, please see the section entitled "Introduction to the SBLGNT."

The *Beginning-Intermediate Greek Readers* for the Catholic Letters (James, 1–2 Peter, 1–3 John, and Jude) will include an additional apparatus at the end of Appendix I that shows any differences between the SBLGNT and ECM (*Novum Testamentum Graecum: Editio Critica Maior*). This short apparatus is from the SBLGNT, which is there titled "Appendix: The SBLGNT in comparison to ECM."

Appendix II: Vocabulary 50 times or more sorted by frequency. In order to best serve the Koinē Greek student, all vocabulary assumed as known has been sorted from most to least frequent and is included in Appendix II. The frequency of occurrence for each word is based upon the SBLGNT and not the NA. These 310 words, which occur 50 times or more in the SBLGNT, are available for students wanting to learn or refresh their basic Greek vocabulary.

Appendix III: Vocabulary 50 times or more arranged alphabetically. All vocabulary occurring 50 times or more in the SBLGNT, which is assumed as known, is arranged alphabetically in Appendix III.

Appendix IV: Koinē Greek Paradigm Charts. These paradigm charts will be a helpful resource to students having difficulty parsing words or just needing a quick reminder about Greek endings. The *Koinē Greek Paradigm Charts* were created by J. Klay Harrison in consultation with Fredrick J. Long.

Introduction to the SBLGNT[1]

The Text

The *SBL Greek New Testament* (SBLGNT) is a new edition of the Greek New Testament, established with the help of earlier editions. In particular, four editions of the Greek New Testament were utilized as primary resources in the process of establishing the SBLGNT. These editions (and their abbreviations) are:

WH Brooke Foss Westcott and Fenton John Anthony Hort, *The New Testament in the Original Greek,* vol. 1: *Text*; vol. 2: *Introduction* [and] *Appendix* (Cambridge: Macmillan, 1881). This justly famous and widely influential nineteenth-century edition of the Greek New Testament was one of the key texts used in the creation of the original Nestle text[2] and was used as the initial basis of comparison in the creation of the United Bible Societies' *Greek New Testament.*[3]

Treg Samuel Prideaux Tregelles, *The Greek New Testament, Edited from Ancient Authorities, with their Various Readings in Full, and the Latin Version of Jerome* (London: Bagster; Stewart, 1857–1879).

---

1 This introduction is a reproduction of the existing introduction written by Michael W. Holmes in the SBLGNT.

2 Eberhard Nestle, *Novum Testamentum Graece* (Stuttgart: Württembergische Bibelanstalt, 1898); cf. the 16th ed. (1936), 38*; cf. also Kurt Aland and Barbara Aland, *The Text of the New Testament* (2nd ed.; trans. E. F. Rhodes; Grand Rapids: Eerdmans; Leiden: Brill, 1989), 19–20.

3 Kurt Aland, Matthew Black, Bruce M. Metzger, and Allen Wikgren, eds., *The Greek New Testament* (New York: American Bible Society; London: British and Foreign Bible Society; Edinburgh: National Bible Society of Scotland; Amsterdam: Netherlands Bible Society; Stuttgart: Württemberg Bible Society, 1966), v.

Although the fine edition of Tregelles has been overshadowed by that of his close contemporaries Westcott and Hort, his textual judgments reveal a "consistency of view and breadth of appreciation" of all the available textual evidence not always as evident in the work of his major nineteenth-century colleagues, who display (to varying degrees) a tendency toward a preoccupation with the latest "big discovery" (Ephraemi Rescriptus/04 in the case of Lachmann, Sinaiticus/01 in the case of Tischendorf, and Vaticanus/03 in the case of Westcott and Hort).[4] Tregelles offers a discerning alternative perspective alongside Westcott and Hort.

NIV Richard J. Goodrich and Albert L. Lukaszewski, *A Reader's Greek New Testament* (Grand Rapids: Zondervan, 2003). This edition presents the Greek text behind the New International Version[5] as reconstructed by Edward Goodrick and John Kohlenberger III.[6] It thus represents the textual choices made by the Committee on Bible Translation, the international group of scholars responsible for the NIV translation. According to its editors, this edition differs from the United Bible Societies/Nestle-Aland editions of the Greek New Testament at 231 places.[7]

RP *The New Testament in the Original Greek: Byzantine Textform 2005*, compiled and arranged by Maurice A.

---

4 David C. Parker, "The Development of the Critical Text of the Epistle of James: From Lachmann to the *Editio Critica Maior*," in *New Testament Textual Criticism and Exegesis: Festschrift J. Delobel* (ed. A. Denaux; BETL 161; Leuven: Leuven University Press and Peeters, 2002), 329.

5 *The Holy Bible, New International Version: New Testament* (Grand Rapids: Zondervan, 1973).

6 A second edition published by the same editors and publisher in 2007 (reviewed and modified by Gordon Fee) presents the Greek text behind the TNIV translation.

7 Goodrich and Lukaszewski, *A Reader's Greek New Testament*, 10 n. 6.

Robinson and William G. Pierpont (Southborough, Mass.: Chilton, 2005). This edition offers a text that is a reliable representative of the Byzantine textual tradition.

Establishing the Text

The starting point for the SBLGNT was the edition of Westcott and Hort. First, the WH text was modified to match the orthographic standards of the SBLGNT (described below). Next, the modified version was compared to the other three primary editions (Treg, NIV, and RP) in order to identify points of agreement and disagreement between them. Where all four editions agreed, the text was tentatively accepted as the text of the SBL edition; points of disagreement were marked for further consideration. The editor then worked systematically through the entire text, giving particular attention to the points of disagreement but examining as well the text where all four editions were in agreement.[8] Where there was disagreement among the four editions, the editor determined which variant to print as the text;[9] occasionally a reading not found in any of the four editions commended itself as the most probable representative of the text and therefore was adopted. Similarly, where all four texts were in agreement, the editor determined whether to accept that reading or to adopt an alternative variant as the text.[10] In this manner, the text of the SBLGNT was established.

---

8 For a brief overview of the editor's methodological and historical perspectives with regard to the practice of New Testament textual criticism, see Michael W. Holmes, "Reconstructing the Text of the New Testament," in *The Blackwell Companion to the New Testament* (ed. David E. Aune; Oxford: Wiley-Blackwell, 2010), 77–89.

9 Or, to put the matter a bit more precisely, which variant most likely represents the form in which the text first began to be copied and to circulate.

10 In all, there are fifty-six variation units in the SBLGNT where the editor preferred a reading not found in any of the four primary editions. In thirty-eight of those instances, the editor's preferred reading is also read by WHmarg (30x) and/or Tregmarg (2x) and/or NA (10x).

A comparison of this new text with the four editions listed above, using as the database the 6,928 variation units recorded in the accompanying apparatus (described below), reveals the following patterns of agreement and difference:

	Agreements	Disagreements
SBL—WH:	6,047	881
SBL—Treg:	5,699	1,229
SBL—NIV:	6,310	618
SBL—RP:	970	5,958

Also interesting is a comparison of agreements of the SBLGNT with one of the four editions against the other three and, vice versa, SBLGNT and the other three against the one:

SBL + WH vs. Treg NIV RP: 99	SBL + Treg NIV RP vs. WH: 365
SBL + Treg vs. WH NIV RP: 28	SBL + WH NIV RP vs. Treg: 150
SBL + NIV vs. WH Treg RP: 59	SBL + WH Treg RP vs. NIV: 103
SBL + RP vs. WH Treg NIV: 66	SBL + WH Treg NIV vs. RP: 4,874

Orthography and Related Matters

The orthography of this edition (including accents and breathings[11]) follows that of the Bauer-Danker-Arndt-Gingrich lexicon (BDAG).[12] This includes both text and apparatus:

11 Occasionally breathings are as much a matter of interpretation as of lexicography. In agreement with a minority of the membership of the UBS Editorial Committee (see Bruce M. Metzger, *A Textual Commentary on The Greek New Testament* [London: United Bible Societies, 1971], 616 [a discussion of Phil 3:21 not found in the second edition]), the SBLGNT occasionally prints a rough breathing on forms of αὑτός.

12 *A Greek-English Lexicon of the New Testament and Other*

entries in the apparatus generally have been conformed to the orthography of BDAG regardless of the spelling of the source edition.

With regard to elision (e.g., ἀλλ' for ἀλλά), crasis (e.g., κἀγώ for καὶ ἐγώ), movable ν, and the interchange between first aorist and second aorist verb endings, the text of Westcott and Hort has been followed. As in the case of orthography, this guideline generally applies to the apparatus as well as the text.

Capitalization

Capitalization follows the pattern of the third edition of *The Apostolic Fathers: Greek Texts and English Translations*,[13] which capitalizes (1) the first word of a paragraph; (2) the first word of direct speech; and (3) proper nouns.[14] Occasionally capitalization in a variant reading in the apparatus may follow that of the source edition.

Early Christian Literature (3rd ed., revised and edited by Frederick William Danker; based on the 6th ed. of Walter Bauer's *Griechisch-deutsches Wörterbuch zu den Schriften des Neuen Testaments und der frühchristlichen Literatur*; Chicago: University of Chicago Press, 2000). Thus ἁγνεία, not ἁγνία (so WH), or, e.g., in the case of words with movable ς (cf. BDF §21), ἄχρι, μέχρι, and οὕτως are printed throughout, unless BDAG indicates otherwise (ἄχρις, Gal 3:19 and Heb 3:13; μέχρις, Mark 13:30, Gal 4:19, Heb 12:4; οὕτω, Acts 23:11, Phil 3:17, Heb 12:21, Rev 16:18). A rare exception to the guideline is the adoption of νουμηνίας rather than νεομηνίας in Col 2:16.

13 Michael W. Holmes, ed., *The Apostolic Fathers: Greek Texts and English Translations* (3rd ed.; Grand Rapids: Baker Academic, 2007).

14 A category that offers, to be sure, numerous opportunities for differences of opinion.

Verse Division, Punctuation, and Paragraphing

The verse divisions follow those of the Nestle-Aland/United Bible Societies Greek texts throughout.[15] Differences between editions have not been recorded.

Punctuation generally follows that of Westcott and Hort. Regular exceptions include instances where a textual decision or the adoption of NRSV paragraphing required a corresponding change in punctuation. Where Westcott and Hort employed two consecutive punctuation marks (such as a comma following or preceding a dash; see 1 Tim 1:5, 2:7), these have been reduced to a single mark. A high point has been added before direct speech if no other punctuation is present. Occasionally other changes have been made as required by context.

Paragraphing generally follows the pattern of the NRSV. Conflicts between NRSV paragraphing and Westcott and Hort punctuation have been resolved on a contextual basis.[16]

Symbols used in the Text

⸀ or ⸀̇ or ⸀1	A textual note pertains to the following word. When identical words in the same verse are marked, the dotted bracket designates the second occurrence. Third (and subsequent) instances are denoted by a numbered bracket to distinguish them from previous instances.
⸂ ⸃ or ⸂̇ ⸃̇	A textual note pertains to the enclosed words.

15 A partial exception occurs at the end of Acts 19, where (in accordance with some editions and many recent translations) a forty-first verse number has been placed in the text, but in brackets ([41]), to indicate uncertainty regarding its status.

16 For example, at the end of Phil 1:18, WH's punctuation was given preference over the NRSV paragraph break, whereas at Phil 2:14 the NRSV paragraphing was followed rather than the WH punctuation (which was changed accordingly).

When identical phrases in the same verse are marked, dotted brackets designate the second occurrence. Similarly, when a second multiword variation unit falls within the boundaries of a longer multiword variation unit, the dotted brackets mark the second occurrence.

[ ] The enclosed text is doubtful.[17]

The Apparatus

The textual apparatus provides information about a wide range of textual variants.[18] It records all differences between the text of the SBLGNT and the texts of WH, Treg, NIV, RP, and NA except for those differences that fall in the category of "orthography and related matters" (discussed above).[19] That is,

---

17 Brackets have been employed in this edition sparingly—not, one hopes, due to a lack of what Parker nicely terms "wise reticence" in the face of difficult choices (Parker, "Development," 325), but for positive reasons. These include a widely shared sense that brackets have been somewhat overused in some recent editions (sometimes as what could be perceived as a means of avoiding difficult choices); an opinion that one of an editor's duties is to make choices, particularly in the "hard cases," so as to offer some degree of guidance to those making use of the resulting text; and a corresponding concern that the availability of brackets biases the decision-making process toward inclusion (one can bracket an included word about which one has some degree of doubt regarding the decision to include it, but one cannot bracket the omission of a word about which one has an equal degree of doubt regarding the decision to exclude it). In all, for better or worse, single brackets appear only six times in the SBLGNT (at Luke 22:19–20; 24:40; 24:51; 24:52; Eph 1:1; Col 1:20).

18 In general, it closely follows the pattern of the apparatus in Holmes, *The Apostolic Fathers* (3rd ed.).

19 This means that the apparatus includes nearly all the variant or alternative readings noted in the margins or notes of most recent major English translations and numerous translations into other languages as well.

the apparatus does not take note of differences that are solely a matter of orthographic variation or that involve only elision, crasis, movable ν, interchange between first and second aorist verb endings, and the like; it does record all other differences between the SBL text and the texts of the five other editions just listed.

The four primary editions (WH Treg NIV RP) are cited for every variation unit (of which there are 6,928).[20] NA is cited only when it differs from NIV. Occasionally a marginal reading of WH or Treg or the text of another edition is cited, usually in support of a reading adopted by the editor that is not found in any of the four primary editions, but sometimes in other circumstances as well.

In each note, the reading of the text is always presented first, in bold, followed by its supporting evidence; the variant reading(s) and supporting evidence follow. Because the different editions use single brackets ([ ]) in the text in different ways, the apparatus does not record details regarding an edition's use of brackets in its text.

Symbols used in the notes

•	Separates multiple variation units within a verse.
]	Separates the reading of the text (and its support) from variant readings.
;	Separates multiple variants within a single variation unit.
+	The following text is added by the listed witness(es).

---

20 For variants involving the verses or parts of verses that WH print between double brackets (⟦ ⟧), WH is cited in the apparatus between brackets (i.e., ⟦WH⟧).

– The indicated text is omitted by the listed witness(es).

⟦ ⟧ Used by Westcott and Hort to mark material that they did not think belonged to the genuine text but that they did not feel free to remove completely from their printed text due to its antiquity or intrinsic interest. When placed around their initials in the apparatus (i.e., ⟦WH⟧), double brackets signal that WH placed them around the text or variant reading in question.

. . . Replaces identical text shared by all the variants in a particular variation unit.

Abbreviations Used in the Notes

ECM *Novum Testamentum Graecum: Editio Critica Maior*, ed. The Institute for New Testament Textual Research, vol. 4: *Catholic Letters*, ed. Barbara Aland, Kurt Aland, Gerd Mink, Holger Strutwolf, and Klaus Wachtel (4 installments; Stuttgart: Deutsche Biblegesellschaft, 1997–2005): inst. 1: *James* (1997; 2nd rev. impr., 1998); inst. 2: *The Letters of Peter* (2000); inst. 3: *The First Letter of John* (2003); inst. 4: *The Second and Third Letter of John, The Letter of Jude* (2005).

em emendation

Greeven Indicates a reading printed as the text by Heinrich Greeven in Albert Huck, *Synopse der drei ersten Evangelien/Synopsis of the*

First Three Gospels (13th ed. fundamentally revised by Heinrich Greeven; Tübingen: Mohr Siebeck), 1981).

Holmes — Indicates a reading preferred by the editor that is not found in any of the four primary editions.

NA — Represents the NA^{26-27}/UBS^{3-4} editions, which all print the identical Greek text. NA is explicitly cited only when it differs from NIV.

NIV — Richard J. Goodrich and Albert L. Lukaszewski, eds., *A Reader's Greek New Testament* (Grand Rapids: Zondervan, 2003).

RP — *The New Testament in the Original Greek: Byzantine Textform 2005*, compiled and arranged by Maurice A. Robinson and William G. Pierpont (Southborough, Mass.: Chilton, 2005).

TR — *Textus Receptus* ("Received Text"). The phrase technically designates the edition of the Greek New Testament printed by the Elziver Brothers in 1633; in generic use it can designate not only the Elziver text but also its precursors (Erasmus, Stephanus, and Beza) or any similar text.[21]

Treg — Samuel Prideaux Tregelles, *The Greek New Testament, Edited from Ancient Authorities,*

---

21 For example, F. H. A. Scrivener, ed., *Η ΚΑΙΝΗ ΔΙΑΘΗΚΗ, Novum Testamentum: Textus Stephanici A.D. 1550* (4th ed., corrected by E. Nestle; London: Bell; Cambridge: Deighton, Bell, 1906) (the printing of the TR consulted for this edition).

	with their Various Readings in Full, and the Latin Version of Jerome (London: Bagster; Stewart, 1857–1879).
Treg^{marg}	Indicates a reading printed by Tregelles in the margin of his edition.
WH	Brooke Foss Westcott and Fenton John Anthony Hort, *The New Testament in the Original Greek,* vol. 1: *Text*; vol. 2: *Introduction* [and] *Appendix* (Cambridge: Macmillan, 1881).
WH^{app}	Indicates a reading discussed by WH in the *Appendix* to their edition (in vol. 2).
WH^{marg}	Indicates an alternative reading printed by WH in the margin of their edition.

Understanding the Apparatus: A Brief Guide

This brief guide supplements what is said above about the apparatus to the SBLGNT by offering further explanation and examples.

The textual apparatus provides a textual note for each of the more than 6,900 instances of variation in the SBLGNT. In each note, the marked reading in the text is always listed first, in bold, and followed immediately by its supporting evidence. The separator bracket (]) comes next, followed by the variant reading(s) and supporting evidence. Multiple variation units in the same verse are separated by a bullet (•), as in all three examples below. Multiple variant readings in the same variation unit are separated by a semicolon (;), as in the second variant in Matt 22:30 below (τοῦ θεοῦ RP; – WH Treg NIV).

Symbols in the text alert the reader to the presence of textual notes in the apparatus. The most frequently used symbols are ⸀ and ⸂ ⸃; the former marks a single word, and the latter encloses a multiple word phrase. If the same word is marked a second time in the same verse, the ⸁ symbol is used to mark the second occurrence (as in Matt 10:28 below, twice). If an identical multiword phrase is marked a second time in the same verse, the ⸄ ⸅ symbols are used to mark the second occurrence (as in John 18:39 below). In both cases, for clarity the symbols are repeated in the textual note. (More complex cases are discussed below.)

Matt 10:28 text:

> 28 καὶ μὴ ⸀φοβεῖσθε ἀπὸ τῶν ἀποκτεννόντων τὸ σῶμα τὴν δὲ ψυχὴν μὴ δυναμένων ἀποκτεῖναι· ⸁φοβεῖσθε δὲ μᾶλλον τὸν δυνάμενον ⸀καὶ ψυχὴν ⸁καὶ σῶμα ἀπολέσαι ἐν γεέννῃ.

> textual note in apparatus:

> **28** ⸀**φοβεῖσθε** Treg NIV RP] φοβηθῆτε WH • ⸁**φοβεῖσθε** WH NIV] φοβήθητε Treg RP • ⸀**καὶ** WH Treg NIV] + τὴν RP • ⸁**καὶ** WH Treg NIV] + τὸ RP

John 18:39 text:

> 39 ἔστιν δὲ συνήθεια ὑμῖν ἵνα ἕνα ⸂ἀπολύσω ὑμῖν⸃ ἐν τῷ πάσχα· βούλεσθε οὖν ⸄ἀπολύσω ὑμῖν⸅ τὸν βασιλέα τῶν Ἰουδαίων;

> textual note in apparatus:

> **39** ⸂**ἀπολύσω ὑμῖν**⸃ WH Treg NIV] ὑμῖν ἀπολύσω RP • ⸄**ἀπολύσω ὑμῖν**⸅ WH Treg NIV] ὑμῖν ἀπολύσω RP

Matt 22:30 text:

> 30 ἐν γὰρ τῇ ἀναστάσει οὔτε γαμοῦσιν οὔτε ⸀γαμίζονται, ἀλλ᾽ ὡς ἄγγελοι ⸀θεοῦ ἐν ⸀τῷ οὐρανῷ εἰσιν·

> textual note in apparatus:

> **30 γαμίζονται** WH Treg NIV] ἐκγαμίζονται RP • **θεοῦ** Holmes] τοῦ θεοῦ RP; – WH Treg NIV • **τῷ** WH Treg NIV] – RP

Variant readings can be one of three types: addition, omission, or substitution. An addition is signaled by the plus sign (+), which indicates that the following word or words are added to the reading of the text by the supporting edition(s) listed after the additional words. In Matt 10:28 above, for example, taking the third and fourth variants together, the SBL text reads καὶ ψυχὴν καὶ σῶμα (with WH Treg NIV), while the RP text—adding τὴν after ⸀καὶ and τὸ after ⸀καὶ —reads καὶ τὴν ψυχὴν καὶ τὸ σῶμα.

An omission is signaled by the minus sign (–) or dash, which indicates that the word(s) marked in the text are omitted by the supporting edition(s) listed after the minus sign. In the second variant in Matt 22:30 above, where the SBL text reads ὡς ἄγγελοι θεοῦ, WH Treg NIV omit the word θεοῦ, and thus read only ὡς ἄγγελοι (see also the last variant in 22:30).

If there is neither a plus nor a minus sign, the variant reading is a substitution: the word(s) marked in the text are replaced by the word(s) in the variant reading by the supporting edition(s) listed after the variant reading. In the first variant in Matt 10:28, for example, the SBL text reads φοβεῖσθε (with Treg NIV RP), while the WH text reads φοβηθῆτε (see also the second variant in this verse, both variants in John 18:39, and the first variant in 22:30).

The above examples cover a very large proportion of the variation units in the apparatus, though more complex cases do sometimes occur. If, for example, the same word is marked more than twice in the same sentence, the symbols ⸀1 and ⸀2 are used for subsequent occurrences (as in 1 Cor 12:10 below, where the same word is marked four times). Occasionally, the ⸄ ⸅ symbols (whose typical use was described above) can also be used to mark a shorter multiword variant that occurs inside a longer multiword variant (see Luke 22:43–44 below). Also, a single-word variant marker (⸀) can occur inside a regular set (⸂ ⸃) of multiple-word variant markers (as in John 13:2 below). A key point to remember when encountering an "opening" multiple-word marker, whether ⸂ or ⸄, is to always look for the corresponding "closing" marker (⸃ or ⸅); this will help to avoid confusion.

1 Cor 12:10 text:

10 ⸀ἄλλῳ ἐνεργήματα δυνάμεων, ⸀ἄλλῳ προφητεία, ⸀1ἄλλῳ διακρίσεις πνευμάτων, ⸀ἑτέρῳ γένη γλωσσῶν, ⸀2ἄλλῳ ἑρμηνεία γλωσσῶν·

textual note in apparatus:

10 ⸀ἄλλῳ Holmes] + δὲ WH Treg NIV RP • **⸀ἄλλῳ** Treg] + δὲ WH NIV RP • **⸀1ἄλλῳ** Treg] + δὲ WH NIV RP • **ἑτέρῳ** WH Treg NIV] + δὲ RP • **⸀2ἄλλῳ** Holmes] + δὲ WH Treg NIV RP

Luke 22.43–44 text:

43 ⸂ὤφθη δὲ αὐτῷ ἄγγελος ⸀ἀπ᾽ οὐρανοῦ ἐνισχύων
αὐτόν. 44 καὶ γενόμενος ἐν ἀγωνίᾳ ἐκτενέστερον
προσηύχετο· ⸄καὶ ἐγένετο⸅ ὁ ἱδρὼς αὐτοῦ ὡσεὶ
θρόμβοι αἵματος καταβαίνοντες ἐπὶ τὴν γῆν.⸃

textual note in apparatus:

43–44 ὤφθη δὲ … ἐπὶ τὴν γῆν. Treg NIV RP] ⟦WH⟧ • **ἀπ'** NIV RP] ἀπὸ τοῦ ⟦WH⟧ Treg • **καὶ ἐγένετο** ⟦WH⟧ NIV] ἐγένετο δὲ Treg RP

Here the symbols ⸂ ⸃ mark off a variant involving the inclusion (by Treg NIV RP) or omission (by WH) of verses 43–44. Within that larger variant, a smaller multiword variant marked by ⸄ ⸅ involves a word-order difference. Since the ⸂ "opening" symbol always is matched by a ⸃ "closing" symbol, and the ⸄ symbol always corresponds with ⸅, it is possible to "nest" the two variants without confusion as to where each begins and ends.

This variant offers an opportunity to comment on the use of another symbol, ⟦WH⟧. There are some verses that Westcott and Hort did not think belonged to the genuine text but that they did not feel free to remove completely from their printed text due to its antiquity or intrinsic interest. In the first entry in the apparatus (**ὤφθη δὲ … ἐπὶ τὴν γῆν.** Treg NIV RP] ⟦WH⟧), the symbol ⟦WH⟧ signals that Westcott and Hort placed verses 43–44 inside double brackets, whereas Treg NIV RP included them in their texts. In the third variant (**καὶ ἐγένετο** ⟦WH⟧ NIV] ἐγένετο δὲ Treg RP), involving a difference in word order, the presence of ⟦WH⟧ signals that Westcott and Hort support the same word order as NIV and reminds us that they did not view the phrase (or the verse of which it is a part) as part of the original text.

John 13.2 text:

2 καὶ δείπνου ⸀γινομένου, τοῦ διαβόλου ἤδη βεβληκότος εἰς τὴν καρδίαν ⸂ἵνα παραδοῖ αὐτὸν Ἰούδας Σίμωνος ⸀Ἰσκαριώτου⸃,

textual note in apparatus:

> 2 **γινομένου** WH Treg NIV] γενομένου RP • **ἵνα παραδοῖ αὐτὸν Ἰούδας Σίμωνος Ἰσκ.** WH Treg NIV] Ἰούδα Σίμωνος Ἰσκ. ἵνα αὐτὸν παραδῷ RP • **Ἰσκαριώτου** NIV RP] Ἰσκαριώτης WH Treg

In this instance, the word-order variation (⸉ἵνα παραδοῖ αὐτὸν Ἰούδας Σίμωνος Ἰσκαριώτου⸊) is unrelated to the separate variant involving the spelling of ⸀Ἰσκαριώτου, so they have been set up as separate variants, the smaller one "nested" inside the larger. The larger variant bounded by the symbols ⸉ ⸊ deals with the word-order variation, while the variant signaled by the ⸀ symbol deals with the spelling variation.

Two other matters call for comment. One is punctuation, which in general is not taken into account in the textual notes. Occasionally, however, a variant may carry with it consequences for how the verse is punctuated. In these cases, punctuation is included in the textual note, as in the second variant in Rev 21:4:

> **4 ἐκ** WH Treg NIV] ἀπὸ RP • **ἔτι.** WH] ἔτι, ὅτι Treg NIV RP

Here the inclusion of ὅτι (supported by Treg NIV RP) alters the syntax of the sentence and so requires a change in punctuation, from the full stop of WH to a comma. The textual note, therefore, indicates both the textual variants and the punctuation that corresponds with them.

The other is the use of ellipsis (…) in the textual notes. Sometimes it is used to save space, especially in variants involving word order. In Matt 15:37 (καὶ ἔφαγον πάντες καὶ ἐχορτάσθησαν, καὶ ⸉τὸ περισσεῦον τῶν κλασμάτων ἦραν⸊ ἑπτὰ σπυρίδας πλήρεις), for example, giving the full text of each variant would result in a textual note like this:

> **37 τὸ περισσεῦον τῶν κλασμάτων ἦραν** WH Treg NIV] ἦραν τὸ περισσεῦον τῶν κλασμάτων RP

The use of ellipses to replace exactly the same words in each variant results in a shorter note:

> **37 τὸ … κλασμάτων ἦραν** WH Treg NIV] ἦραν τὸ … κλασμάτων RP.

In other cases the use of ellipses helps to make clear the places where two or more textual variants actually differ. In Acts 9:31, for example, the entire verse is enclosed by a pair of multiword variant markers (31 ⸂μὲν οὖν ἐκκλησία καθ' ὅλης τῆς Ἰουδαίας καὶ Γαλιλαίας καὶ Σαμαρείας εἶχεν εἰρήνην οἰκοδομουμένη, καὶ πορευομένη τῷ φόβῳ τοῦ κυρίου καὶ τῇ παρακλήσει τοῦ ἁγίου πνεύματος ἐπληθύνετο⸃). The apparatus, however, looks like this:

> **31 Ἡ … ἐκκλησία … εἶχεν … οἰκοδομουμένη … πορευομένη … ἐπληθύνετο** WH Treg NIV] Αἱ … ἐκκλησίαι … εἶχον … οἰκοδομούμεναι … πορευόμεναι … ἐπληθύνοντο RP

Here the ellipses not only save space but also reveal clearly the places where the variant readings differ and the nature of the variation (singular versus plural).

ΙΑΚΩΒΟΥ

JAMES 1

NEW VOCABULARY BY FREQUENCY

[Chapter, Book, SBLGNT Occurrences]

θλῖψις, -εως, ἡ, *affliction, persecution* [1, 1, 45]
Ἰάκωβος, ου, ὁ, *James* [1, 1, 42]
ἐργάζομαι, *I work, perform, accomplish* [1, 2, 41]
πειράζω, *I attempt; I test, tempt* [4, 4, 39]
πλανάω, *I lead astray* [1, 2, 39]
ἐπιθυμία, -ας, ἡ, *eager desire, passion, lust* [2, 2, 38]
βούλομαι, *I wish; I intend* [1, 3, 37]
καυχάομαι, *I boast, am proud of* [1, 2, 36]
ὀργή, -ῆς, ἡ, *anger, wrath* [2, 2, 36]
εὐθέως, *immediately* [1, 1, 35]
ἥλιος, -ου, ὁ, *the sun* [1, 1, 32]
ὑπομονή, -ῆς, ἡ, *patient endurance, perseverance* [2, 3, 32]
φυλη, -ῆς, ἡ, *tribe, nation* [1, 1, 31]
παρέρχομαι, *I go by, pass by; I pass away* [1, 1, 29]
ἡγέομαι, *I lead, guide; I consider* [1, 1, 28]
πλούσιος, -α, -ον, *rich, wealthy* [2, 5, 28]
καθαρός, -ά, -όν, *clean, pure, innocent* [1, 1, 26]
χήρα, -ας, ἡ, *widow* [1, 1, 26]
κατεργάζομαι, *I accomplish, bring about; I produce* [1, 1, 22]
πειρασμός, -οῦ, ὁ, *temptation, test* [2, 2, 21]
διακρίνω, *I discriminate, judge; I doubt (middle)* [2, 3, 19]
τέλειος, -α, -ον, *perfect, complete, mature* [4, 5, 19]
στέφανος, -ου, ὁ, *crown, wreath* [1, 1, 18]
τίκτω, *I give birth to* [1, 1, 18]
ὑπομένω, *I tarry, endure* [1, 2, 17]
συλλαμβάνω, *I take, conceive* [1, 1, 16]
εἶτα, *then* [1, 1, 15]
ἐπαγγέλλομαι, *I promise* [1, 2, 15]
ξηραίνω, *to dry up* [1, 1, 15]
χόρτος, -ου, ὁ, *grass, hay* [2, 2, 15]
κατανοέω, *I observe* [2, 2, 14]

ἄνωθεν, *from above, again* [1, 3, 13]
ταχύς, -εῖα, *quickly, quick* [1, 1, 13]
ἐλευθερία, -ας, ἡ, *liberty* [1, 2, 11]
ἐπισκέπτομαι, *I visit, have a care for* [1, 1, 11]
κακία, -ας, ἡ, *malice, evil* [1, 1, 11]
πραΰτης, -ητος, ἡ, *gentleness, humility, courtesy* [1, 2, 11]
ἐκπίπτω, *to fall away* [1, 1, 10]
ὀνειδίζω, *I reproach* [1, 1, 10]
ποικίλος, -η, -ον, *varied, manifold* [1, 1, 10]
ἀνατέλλω, trans., *I cause to rise;* intrans., *I rise* [1, 1, 9]
ἀπαρχή, -ῆς, ἡ, *the first fruit* [1, 1, 9]
ἀποτίθημι, *I put off, lay aside* [1, 1, 8]
ἐπιλανθάνομαι, *I forget, neglect* [1, 1, 8]
ταπεινός, -ή, -όν, *humble, downcast* [1, 2, 8]
δόκιμος, -ον, *tested, approved* [1, 1, 7]
ἔνι, *there is* [1, 1, 6]
λείπω, *I leave, leave behind; I lack* [2, 3, 6]
μάταιος, -α, -ον, *vain, useless, worthless* [1, 1, 6]
ποιητής, -οῦ, ὁ, *a maker, a doer* [3, 4, 6]
ὕψος, -ους, τό, *height* [1, 1, 6]
γένεσις, -εως, ἡ, *origin, birth, genealogy* [1, 2, 5]
ὁποῖος, -α, -ον, *what sort of, what kind of* [1, 1, 5]
παρακύπτω, *I stoop to look, I look* [1, 1, 5]
ἀκροατής, -οῦ, ὁ, *a hearer* [3, 3, 4]
ἀμίαντος, -ον, *undefiled* [1, 1, 4]
ἄνθος, -ους, τό, *a flower* [2, 2, 4]
ἄσπιλος, -ον, *spotless, unstained* [1, 1, 4]
θρησκεία, -ας, ἡ, *religion, worship* [2, 2, 4]
κτίσμα, -τος, τό, *a creature* [1, 1, 4]
παραμένω, *I remain beside, continue, abide* [1, 1, 4]
περισσεία, -ας, ἡ, *superfluity, surplus, abundance* [1, 1, 4]
ταπείνωσις, -εως, ἡ, *humiliation, humble state* [1, 1, 4]
ἀπατάω, *I deceive* [1, 1, 3]
βραδύς, -εῖα, -ύ, *slow* [2, 2, 3]
δελεάζω, *I lure, entice* [1, 1, 3]
διασπορά, -ᾶς, ἡ, *diaspora, a dispersion* [1, 1, 3]
καύσων, -ωνος, ὁ, *burning heat* [1, 1, 3]

οἴομαι, *I suppose, expect, think* [1, 1, 3]
περιπίπτω, *I fall in with, strike* [1, 1, 3]
ἀκατάστατος, -ον, *unstable, restless* [1, 2, 2]
ἀποκυέω, *I give birth to, bring forth* [2, 2, 2]
ἀποτελέω, *I bring to completion, finish, perform* [1, 1, 2]
δίψυχος, -ον, *double-minded, hesitating* [1, 2, 2]
δοκίμιον, -ου, τό, *a testing* [1, 1, 2]
δόσις, -εως, ἡ, *gift, giving* [1, 1, 2]
δώρημα, -τος, τό, *a gift, present* [1, 1, 2]
ἔοικα, *to be like* [2, 2, 2]
ἔσοπτρον, -ου, τό, *a mirror* [1, 1, 2]
κλύδων, -ωνος, ὁ, *rough water, a wave* [1, 1, 2]
ὁλόκληρος, -ον, *whole, complete* [1, 1, 2]
ὀρφανός, -ή, -όν, *an orphan* [1, 1, 2]
παραλογίζομαι, *I deceive, delude* [1, 1, 2]
πορεία, -ας, ἡ, *a journey, way, pursuit* [1, 1, 2]
χαλιναγωγέω, *I bridle, hold in check* [1, 2, 2]
ἀνεμίζομαι, *to be driven by the wind* [1, 1, 1]
ἀπείραστος, -ον, *unable to be tempted* [1, 1, 1]
ἁπλῶς, *simply, sincerely, generously* [1, 1, 1]
ἀποσκίασμα, -τος, τό, *a shadow* [1, 1, 1]
ἔμφυτος, -ον, *implanted* [1, 1, 1]
ἐξέλκω, *I drag away* [1, 1, 1]
ἐπιλησμονή, -ῆς, ἡ, *forgetfulness* [1, 1, 1]
εὐπρέπεια, -ας, ἡ, *beauty, loveliness* [1, 1, 1]
θρησκός, -όν, *religious* [1, 1, 1]
μαραίνομαι, *I die out, fade away* [1, 1, 1]
παραλλαγή, -ῆς, ἡ, *a change, variation* [1, 1, 1]
ποίησις, -εως, ἡ, *a making, a doing* [1, 1, 1]
ῥιπίζομαι, *to be tossed about by the wind* [1, 1, 1]
ῥυπαρία, -ας, ἡ, *filthiness, vulgarity* [1, 1, 1]
τροπή, -ῆς, ἡ, *a turning, change* [1, 1, 1]

ΙΑΚΩΒΟΥ

1.1 Ἰάκωβος[1] θεοῦ καὶ κυρίου Ἰησοῦ Χριστοῦ δοῦλος
ταῖς δώδεκα φυλαῖς[2] ταῖς ἐν τῇ διασπορᾷ[3] χαίρειν[4].

2 Πᾶσαν χαρὰν ἡγήσασθε[5], ἀδελφοί μου, ὅταν
πειρασμοῖς[6] περιπέσητε[7] ποικίλοις[8], **3** γινώσκοντες[9] ὅτι
τὸ δοκίμιον[10] ὑμῶν τῆς πίστεως κατεργάζεται[11]
ὑπομονήν.[12] **4** ἡ δὲ ὑπομονὴ[13] ἔργον τέλειον[14] ἐχέτω[15], ἵνα
ἦτε τέλειοι[16] καὶ ὁλόκληροι[17], ἐν μηδενὶ λειπόμενοι[18].

---

[1] Ἰάκωβος, ου, ὁ, *James.*

[2] φυλη, -ῆς, ἡ, *tribe, nation.*

[3] διασπορά, -ᾶς, ἡ, *diaspora, a dispersion.*

[4] TH: χαίρειν inf. abs. frequently used as a formal greeting outside NT, *greetings.*

[5] ἡγέομαι, *I lead, guide;* ***I consider***. TH: aor. mid. impv. 2nd pl.

[6] πειρασμός, -οῦ, ὁ, *temptation, test;* ***trial***. TH: dat. complement of περιπέσητε.

[7] περιπίπτω, *I fall in with, strike;* ***I encounter***. MH: aor. act. subj. 2nd pl. from cmpd. verb περιπίπτω = pref. (περί) + root + tense formative + 2nd pl. act. ending (περι + πε + σα + τε). Vowel in tense formative (σα) lengthens in subj. mood (ση).

[8] ποικίλος, -η, -ον, *varied, manifold.* TH: modifier separated from πειρασμοῖς, *various trials.*

[9] TH: γινώσκοντες, an adv. causal prtc., modifying ἡγήσασθε, *because you know.*

[10] δοκίμιον, -ου, τό, *a testing.*

[11] κατεργάζομαι, *I accomplish, bring about;* ***I produce***.

[12] ὑπομονή, -ῆς, ἡ, *patient endurance, perseverance.*

[13] ὑπομονή, -ῆς, ἡ, *patient endurance, perseverance.*

[14] τέλειος, -α, -ον, *perfect, complete, mature*; TH: ἔργον τέλειον, ***full effect, complete work.***

[15] TH: pres. act. impv. 3rd sg. from ἔχω, *let endurance have* (ὑπομονή = sg. subject).

[16] τέλειος, -α, -ον, *perfect, complete, mature.*

[17] ὁλόκληρος, -ον, *whole, complete.*

[18] λείπω, *I leave, leave behind;* ***I lack***. TH: prtc. of result, *lacking in nothing.*

5 Εἰ δέ τις ὑμῶν λείπεται[1] σοφίας, αἰτείτω παρὰ τοῦ
διδόντος[2] θεοῦ πᾶσιν ἁπλῶς[3] καὶ ⸀μὴ ὀνειδίζοντος[4], καὶ
δοθήσεται [5] αὐτῷ· **6** αἰτείτω [6] δὲ ἐν πίστει, μηδὲν
διακρινόμενος[7], ὁ γὰρ διακρινόμενος[8] ἔοικεν[9] κλύδωνι[10]
θαλάσσης ἀνεμιζομένῳ [11] καὶ ῥιπιζομένῳ [12]. **7** μὴ γὰρ
οἰέσθω[13] ὁ ἄνθρωπος ἐκεῖνος ὅτι λήμψεταί[14] τι παρὰ τοῦ
κυρίου **8** ἀνὴρ δίψυχος[15], ἀκατάστατος[16] ἐν πάσαις ταῖς
ὁδοῖς αὐτοῦ.

---

[1] λείπω, *I leave, leave behind;* ***I lack***.

[2] TH: attrib. prtc. modifying θεοῦ, *the God who gives.*

[3] ἁπλῶς, *simply, sincerely, generously.*

[4] ὀνειδίζω, *I reproach.*

[5] MH: fut. pass. subj. 3rd sg. from δίδωμι = root + tense formative + connecting vowel + 3rd sg. pass. ending (δο + θησ + ε + ται).

[6] TH: pres. act. impv. 3rd sg. from αἰτέω.

[7] διακρίνω, *I discriminate, judge;* ***I doubt (middle)***.

[8] διακρίνω, *I discriminate, judge;* ***I doubt (middle)***. TH: ὁ … διακρινόμενος is subst. prtc., *the one doubting.*

[9] ἔοικα, *to be like.* TH: pf. tense with a pres. meaning and takes a dat. compliment (here, κλύδωνι).

[10] κλύδων, -ωνος, ὁ, *rough water, a wave.*

[11] ἀνεμίζω, *to be driven by the wind.* TH: att. prtc. modifying κλύδωνι.

[12] ῥιπίζω, *to be tossed about by the wind.* TH: att. prtc. modifying κλύδωνι; ἀνεμιζομένῳ καὶ ῥιπιζομένῳ, *driven and tossed by the wind.*

[13] οἴομαι, *I suppose, expect, think.* MH: pres. mid. impv. 3rd sg. from οἴομαι = root + connecting vowel + 3rd sg. mid./pass. ending (οἰ + έ + σθω).

[14] MH: fut. mid. indic. 3rd sg. from λαμβάνω = root + tense formative + connecting vowel + 3rd sg. mid./pass. ending (λημβ + σ + ε + ται). Review Square of Stops, β + σ › ψ.

[15] δίψυχος, -ον, *double-minded, hesitating.*

[16] ἀκατάστατος, -ον, *unstable, restless.*

9 Καυχάσθω[1] δὲ ὁ ἀδελφὸς ὁ ταπεινὸς[2] ἐν τῷ ὕψει[3]
αὐτοῦ, **10** ὁ δὲ πλούσιος[4] ἐν τῇ ταπεινώσει[5] αὐτοῦ, ὅτι ὡς
ἄνθος[6] χόρτου[7] παρελεύσεται[8]. **11** ἀνέτειλεν[9] γὰρ ὁ ἥλιος[10]
σὺν τῷ καύσωνι[11] καὶ ἐξήρανεν[12] τὸν χόρτον[13], καὶ τὸ
ἄνθος[14] αὐτοῦ ἐξέπεσεν[15] καὶ ἡ εὐπρέπεια[16] τοῦ προσώπου
αὐτοῦ ἀπώλετο[17]. οὕτως καὶ ὁ πλούσιος[18] ἐν ταῖς
πορείαις[19] αὐτοῦ μαρανθήσεται[20].

---

[1] καυχάομαι, *I boast, am proud of.* TH: pres. mid./pass. impv. 3rd sg.
[2] ταπεινός, -ή, -όν, *humble, downcast.*
[3] ὕψος, -ους, τό, *height.*
[4] πλούσιος, -α, -ον, *rich, wealthy*. TH: Nom. subject of implied verb, καυχάομαι, *I boast, am proud of.*
[5] ταπείνωσις, -εως, ἡ, *humiliation, humble state.*
[6] ἄνθος, -ους, τό, *a flower.*
[7] χόρτος, -ου, ὁ, *grass, hay;* ***field, meadow***. TH: Adjective χόρτου attrib. to ἄνθος, *a flower of the field, wild flower.*
[8] παρέρχομαι, *I go by, pass by;* ***I pass away***. MH: fut. mid. indic. 3rd sg. = pref. (παρά) + root + tense formative + connecting vowel + 3rd sg. mid./pass. ending (παρα + ελευ + σ + ε + ται). Pref. ending in a vowel (παρά) drops the final vowel because the verbal root begins with a vowel (-ελευσεται).
[9] ἀνατέλλω, trans., *I cause to rise;* intrans., ***I rise***.
[10] ἥλιος, -ου, ὁ, *the sun.*
[11] καύσων, -ωνος, ὁ, *burning heat.*
[12] ξηραίνω, *to dry up*. TH: ἥλιος the subject of both indic. verbs in the clause.
[13] χόρτος, -ου, ὁ, *grass, hay.*
[14] ἄνθος, -ους, τό, *a flower.*
[15] ἐκπίπτω, *I fall away*. MH: aor. act. indic. 3rd sg. from ἐκπίπτω = pref. (ἐξ) + aug. + root + tense formative + 3rd sg. act. ending (ἐξ + ε + πε + σε + ν).
[16] εὐπρέπεια, -ας, ἡ, *beauty, loveliness.*
[17] ἀπόλλυμι, *I destroy; I perish (middle)*. MH: aor. mid. indic. 3rd sg. from ἀπόλλυμι = root + connecting vowel + 3rd sg. mid. ending (ἀπώλ + ε + το). The pres. sg. stem vowel of a μι verb lengthens (ο › ω).
[18] πλούσιος, -α, -ον, *rich, wealthy.*
[19] πορεία, -ας, ἡ, *a journey, way, pursuit.*
[20] μαραίνομαι, *I die out, fade away*. TH: Subject, πλούσιος, is separated by the adv. phrase, ἐν ταῖς πορείαις αὐτοῦ, modifying the verb μαρανθήσεται, fut.

12 Μακάριος ἀνὴρ [1] ὃς ὑπομένει [2] πειρασμόν [3], ὅτι
δόκιμος [4] γενόμενος [5] λήμψεται [6] τὸν στέφανον [7] τῆς ζωῆς, [8]
ὃν ⸀ἐπηγγείλατο [9] τοῖς ἀγαπῶσιν αὐτόν. **13** μηδεὶς
πειραζόμενος [10] λεγέτω ὅτι [11] Ἀπὸ [12] θεοῦ πειράζομαι [13].
ὁ γὰρ θεὸς ἀπείραστός [14] ἐστιν κακῶν [15], πειράζει [16] δὲ
αὐτὸς [17] οὐδένα. **14** ἕκαστος δὲ πειράζεται [18] ὑπὸ τῆς
ἰδίας ἐπιθυμίας [19] ἐξελκόμενος [20] καὶ δελεαζόμενος [21].

---

pass. translated with the active sense, *the rich man in the midst of his pursuit will fade away.*

[1] TH: Pred. adj. μάκαριος in equative clause with nom. subject ἀνήρ, *blessed is the man.*

[2] ὑπομένω, *I tarry, endure.*

[3] πειρασμός, -οῦ, ὁ, *temptation, test.*

[4] δόκιμος, -ον, *tested, approved.*

[5] TH: aor. mid. prtc. nom. masc. sg. from γίνομαι, temporal prtc. ante. to the main verb λήμψεται, *after he has become approved, he will receive.*

[6] MH: fut. mid. indic. 3rd sg. from λαμβάνω = root + tense formative + connecting vowel + 3rd sg. mid./pass. ending (λημβ + σ + ε + ται). Review Square of Stops, β + σ › ψ.

[7] στέφανος, -ου, ὁ, *crown, wreath.*

[8] TH: τῆς ζωῆς = epex. gen., *crown, that is life.*

[9] ἐπαγγέλλομαι, *I promise*. TH: Implied subj., ὁ θεός (see 2:5).

[10] πειράζω, *I attempt; I test, tempt.*

[11] TH: ὅτι introduces dir. discourse that is represented by quotation marks in English.

[12] TH: ἀπό + gen. can mean source and imply agency, *by God.*

[13] πειράζω, *I attempt; I test, tempt.*

[14] ἀπείραστος, -ον, *unable to be tempted.*

[15] TH: gen. pl. neut. from κακός, *evil.* TH: Gen. of means separated from what it modifies: ἀπείραστός … κακῶν, *unable to be tempted by evil.*

[16] πειράζω, *I attempt; I test, tempt.*

[17] TH: Emphatic use of pron., *he himself.*

[18] πειράζω, *I attempt; I test, tempt.*

[19] ἐπιθυμία, -ας, ἡ, *passion, lust,* ***desire***. TH: functions here as a personified agent.

[20] ἐξέλκω, *I drag away.* TH: adv. prtc. placed after main verb to further explain it.

[21] δελεάζω, *I lure, entice.* TH: adv. prtc. placed after main verb to further explain it.

15 εἶτα[1] ἡ ἐπιθυμία[2] συλλαβοῦσα[3] τίκτει[4] ἁμαρτίαν, ἡ δὲ
ἁμαρτία ἀποτελεσθεῖσα[5] ἀποκύει[6] θάνατον. 16 μὴ
πλανᾶσθε[7], ἀδελφοί μου ἀγαπητοί.

17 Πᾶσα δόσις[8] ἀγαθὴ καὶ πᾶν δώρημα[9] τέλειον[10]
ἄνωθέν[11] ἐστιν, καταβαῖνον ἀπὸ τοῦ πατρὸς τῶν φώτων,
παρ' ᾧ οὐκ ἔνι[12] παραλλαγὴ[13] ἢ τροπῆς[14] ἀποσκίασμα[15].
18 βουληθεὶς[16] ἀπεκύησεν[17] ἡμᾶς λόγῳ ἀληθείας, εἰς τὸ
εἶναι ἡμᾶς ἀπαρχήν[18] τινα τῶν αὐτοῦ κτισμάτων[19].

---

[1] εἶτα, *then.*

[2] ἐπιθυμία, -ας, ἡ, *eager desire, passion, lust,* ***desire***.

[3] συλλαμβάνω, *I take, conceive.* TH: Temporal prtc., *after lust conceives, it gives birth to sin.*

[4] τίκτω, *I give birth to.*

[5] ἀποτελέω, *I bring to completion, finish, perform.* TH: Temporal prtc., *After sin is brought to completion, it gives birth to death.*

[6] ἀποκυέω, *I give birth to, bring forth.*

[7] πλανάω, *I lead astray.* TH: pres. pass. impv. 2nd pl.

[8] δόσις, -εως, ἡ, *gift, giving.*

[9] δώρημα, -τος, τό, *a gift, present.*

[10] τέλειος, -α, -ον, *perfect, complete, mature.*

[11] ἄνωθεν, *from above, again.*

[12] ἔνι, *there is.* TH: Shortened form of ἔνεστιν, pres. act. indic. 3rd sg from ἔνειμι.

[13] παραλλαγή, -ῆς, ἡ, *a change, variation.*

[14] τροπή, -ῆς, ἡ, *a turning, change.*

[15] ἀποσκίασμα, -τος, τό, *a shadow.*

[16] βούλομαι, *I wish, I intend.*

[17] ἀποκυέω, *I give birth to, bring forth.* MH: aor. act. indic. 3rd sg. from ἀποκυέω = pref. (ἀπό) + aug. + root + lengthened contract vowel + tense formative + 3rd sg. act. ending (ἀπ + ε + κύ + η + σε + ν). The final vowel in the pref. is dropped due the verbal aug. The vowel in a contract verb is lengthened before the tense formative (ε › η).

[18] ἀπαρχή, -ῆς, ἡ, *the first fruit.*

[19] κτίσμα, -τος, τό, *a creature.*

19 ⸀Ἴστε, ἀδελφοί μου ἀγαπητοί. ἔστω[1] ⸀δὲ πᾶς
ἄνθρωπος ταχὺς[2] εἰς τὸ ἀκοῦσαι[3], βραδὺς[4] εἰς τὸ λαλῆσαι[5],
βραδὺς[6] εἰς ὀργήν[7], **20** ὀργὴ[8] γὰρ ἀνδρὸς δικαιοσύνην θεοῦ
⸂οὐκ ἐργάζεται[9]⸃. **21** διὸ ἀποθέμενοι[10] πᾶσαν ῥυπαρίαν[11] καὶ
περισσείαν[12] κακίας[13] ἐν πραΰτητι[14] δέξασθε[15] τὸν
ἔμφυτον[16] λόγον τὸν δυνάμενον[17] σῶσαι[18] τὰς ψυχὰς ὑμῶν.
22 Γίνεσθε[19] δὲ ποιηταὶ[20] λόγου[21] καὶ μὴ ⸀ἀκροαταὶ[22]

---

[1] TH: pres. act. impv. 3rd sg. from εἰμί, *let every man be.*
[2] ταχύς, -εῖα, *quickly, quick.*
[3] TH: εἰς + articular infinitive typically denotes purpose or result, but in this case can be rendered, *with regard to listening.*
[4] βραδύς, -εῖα, -ύ, *slow.*
[5] TH: εἰς + articular infinitive typically denotes purpose or result, but in this case can be rendered, *with regard to speaking.*
[6] βραδύς, -εῖα, -ύ, *slow.*
[7] ὀργή, -ῆς, ἡ, *anger, wrath.* TH: εἰς + noun breaks the pattern of εἰς + articular infinitive, but carries the similar meaning of respect/reference, *with respect to anger.*
[8] ὀργή, -ῆς, ἡ, *anger, wrath.*
[9] ἐργάζομαι, *I work, perform, accomplish.* NA[28] has οὐ κατεργάζεται.
[10] ἀποτίθημι, *I put off, lay aside.* MH: aor. mid. prtc. nom. masc. pl. from ἀποτίθημι = pref. (ἀπο) + root + mid./pass. prtc. morpheme + nom. masc. pl. case ending (ἀπο +θέ + μεν + οι).
[11] ῥυπαρία, -ας, ἡ, *filthiness, vulgarity.*
[12] περισσεία, -ας, ἡ, *superfluity, surplus, abundance.*
[13] κακία, -ας, ἡ, *malice, evil.*
[14] πραΰτης, -ητος, ἡ, *gentleness, humility, courtesy.*
[15] TH: aor. mid. impv. 2nd pl. from δέχομαι, *(you) receive.*
[16] ἔμφυτος, -ον, *implanted.*
[17] TH: pres. mid./pass. prtc. acc. masc. sg. from δύναμαι. Adjectival prtc. functioning attrib. to τὸν λόγον, *the word which is able.*
[18] TH: Complementary inf. completing the prec. prtc., *which is able to save.*
[19] TH: pres. mid./pass. impv. 2nd pl. from γίνομαι.
[20] ποιητής, -οῦ, ὁ, *a maker, a doer.* TH: Pl. noun as pred. nom., *Be doers.*
[21] TH: Objective gen., *doers of the word.*
[22] ἀκροατής, -οῦ, ὁ, *a hearer.* NA has μόνον ἀκροαταί.

μόνον παραλογιζόμενοι[1] ἑαυτούς. 23 ὅτι εἴ τις ἀκροατὴς[2]
λόγου ἐστὶν καὶ οὐ ποιητής[3], οὗτος ἔοικεν[4] ἀνδρὶ[5]
κατανοοῦντι[6] τὸ πρόσωπον τῆς γενέσεως[7] αὐτοῦ ἐν
ἐσόπτρῳ[8], 24 κατενόησεν[9] γὰρ ἑαυτὸν καὶ ἀπελήλυθεν[10]
καὶ εὐθέως[11] ἐπελάθετο[12] ὁποῖος[13] ἦν. 25 ὁ δὲ παρακύψας[14]
εἰς νόμον τέλειον[15] τὸν τῆς ἐλευθερίας[16] καὶ παραμείνας[17],

---

[1] παραλογίζομαι, *I deceive, delude.*

[2] ἀκροατής, -οῦ, ὁ, *a hearer*. TH: ἀκροατής functions as the predicate nom. of the verb ἐστὶν.

[3] ποιητής, -οῦ, ὁ, *a maker, a doer.*

[4] ἔοικα, *to be like.*

[5] TH: Dat. complement of ἔοικεν.

[6] κατανοέω, *I observe*. TH: pres. act. prtc. dat. masc. sg. Adjectival prtc. functioning attrib. to ἀνδρὶ, *a man who observes.*

[7] γένεσις, -εως, ἡ, *origin, birth, genealogy*. TH: there is no obvious way to translate τὸ πρόσωπον τῆς γενέσεως which literally would mean *the face of the source* or *the face of the birth*, perhaps *his natural face* or simply h*is own face.*

[8] ἔσοπτρον, -ου, τό, *a mirror.*

[9] κατανοέω, *I observe.*

[10] MH: pf. act. indic. 3rd sg. from ἀπέρχομαι = pref. (ἀπό) + root + 3rd sg. act. ending (ἀπ + ελήλυθε + ν). Pref. ending in a vowel (ἀπό) drops the final vowel because the verbal root begins with a vowel (-ελήλυθεν).

[11] εὐθέως, *immediately.*

[12] ἐπιλανθάνομαι, *I forget, neglect*. MH: aor. mid. indic. 3rd sg. from ἐπιλανθάνομαι = pref. (ἐπί) + aug. + root + connecting vowel + 3rd sg. mid. ending (ἐπ + ε + λάθ + ε + το). Pref. ending in a vowel (ἐπί) drops the final vowel because the verbal root is preceded by an aug.

[13] ὁποῖος, -α, -ον, *what sort of, what kind of.*

[14] παρακύπτω, *I stoop to look, to look*. MH: aor. act. prtc. nom. masc. sg. TH: functioning substantivally, *the one who looks.*

[15] τέλειος, -α, -ον, *perfect, complete, mature.*

[16] ἐλευθερία, -ας, ἡ, *liberty.*

[17] παραμένω, *I remain beside, continue, abide*. TH: aor. act. prtc. nom. masc. sg. from παραμένω. Functioning substantivally, *the one who remains.*

⸀οὐκ ἀκροατὴς[1] ἐπιλησμονῆς[2] γενόμενος ἀλλὰ ποιητὴς[3]
ἔργου, οὗτος[4] μακάριος[5] ἐν τῇ ποιήσει[6] αὐτοῦ ἔσται.
26 Εἴ[7] τις δοκεῖ θρησκὸς[8] ⸀εἶναι[9] μὴ χαλιναγωγῶν[10]
γλῶσσαν ⸀αὐτοῦ ἀλλὰ ἀπατῶν[11] καρδίαν ⸀αὐτοῦ, τούτου[12]
μάταιος[13] ἡ θρησκεία[14]. **27** θρησκεία[15] καθαρὰ[16] καὶ
ἀμίαντος[17] παρὰ[18] ⸀τῷ θεῷ καὶ πατρὶ αὕτη[19] ἐστίν,
ἐπισκέπτεσθαι[20] ὀρφανοὺς[21] καὶ χήρας[22] ἐν τῇ θλίψει[23]
αὐτῶν, ἄσπιλον[24] ἑαυτὸν τηρεῖν[25] ἀπὸ τοῦ κόσμου.

---

1 ἀκροατής, -οῦ, ὁ, *a hearer.*
2 ἐπιλησμονή, -ῆς, ἡ, *forgetfulness.*
3 ποιητής, -οῦ, ὁ, *a maker, a doer.*
4 TH: Nom. subj. of ἔσται, *this one will be.*
5 TH: Pred. adj. of ἔσται, *will be blessed.*
6 ποίησις, -εως, ἡ, *a making, a doing.*
7 TH: Introducing a first class condition (assumed true for sake of argument).
8 θρησκός, -όν, *religious.* TH: Pred. adj. of εἶναι.
9 TH: pres. act. inf. from εἰμί. Complementary inf., *if anyone thinks to be.*
10 χαλιναγωγέω, *I bridle, hold in check.*
11 ἀπατάω, *I deceive.*
12 TH: Introduces apodosis of the first class condition, *then this one's religion.*
13 μάταιος, -α, -ον, *vain, useless, worthless.* TH: Pred. adj. of implied equative verb.
14 θρησκεία, -ας, ἡ, *religion, worship.* TH: Nom. subj. of implied equative verb, *this one's religion (is) useless.*
15 θρησκεία, -ας, ἡ, *religion, worship.*
16 καθαρός, -ά, -όν, *clean, pure, innocent.*
17 ἀμίαντος, -ον, *undefiled.*
18 TH: παρὰ + dat., *in the sight of.*
19 TH: Nom. subject of ἐστίν.
20 ἐπισκέπτομαι, *I visit, have a care for.* TH: pres. mid./pass. inf. in app. to αὕτη answering the question "What is pure and undefiled religion in the sight of God?"
21 ὀρφανός, -ή, -όν, *an orphan.*
22 χήρα, -ας, ἡ, *widow.*
23 θλῖψις, -εως, ἡ, *affliction, persecution.*
24 ἄσπιλος, -ον, *spotless, unstained.*
25 TH: pres. act. inf. from τηρέω. in app. to αὕτη answering the question "What is pure and undefiled religion in the sight of God?"

SBLGNT Sigla Apparatus for James 1

⸀ **1:5 μὴ** WH Treg NA28] οὐκ RP
⸀ **12 ἐπηγγείλατο** WH Treg NA28] + ὁ κύριος RP
⸀ **19 Ἴστε** WH Treg NA28] Ὥστε RP
⸀ • **δὲ** WH Treg NA28] – RP
⸂ **20 οὐκ ἐργάζεται** WH Treg NA27] οὐ κατεργάζεται NA28 RP
⸃ **20 οὐκ ἐργάζεται** WH Treg NA27] οὐ κατεργάζεται NA28 RP
⸂ **22 ἀκροαταὶ μόνον** WH Treg] μόνον ἀκροαταὶ NA28 RP
⸃ **22 ἀκροαταὶ μόνον** WH Treg] μόνον ἀκροαταὶ NA28 RP
⸀ **25 οὐκ** WH Treg NA28] οὗτος οὐκ RP
⸀ **26 εἶναι** WH Treg NA28] + ἐν ὑμῖν RP
⸀ • **αὐτοῦ** Treg NA28 RP] ἑαυτοῦ WH
⸀ • **αὐτοῦ** Treg NA28 RP] ἑαυτοῦ WH
⸀ **27 τῷ** WH Treg NA28] – RP

JAMES 2

NEW VOCABULARY BY FREQUENCY

[Chapter, Book, SBLGNT Occurrences]

κρίσις, -εως, ἡ, *judging, trial, judgment* [2, 3, 47]
σεαυτοῦ, -ῆς, *of yourself* [1, 1, 43]
χωρίς, (gen.) *without, apart from* [4, 4, 42]
ἐργάζομαι, *I work, perform, accomplish* [1, 2, 41]
λογίζομαι, *I reckon, consider, think, count* [1, 1, 40]
δικαιόω, *I set right, I justify, to consider righteous* [3, 3, 39]
καλῶς, *well, beautifully* [3, 3, 37]
ὥσπερ, *just as* [1, 1, 36]
βλασφημέω, *I revile sacred things, blaspheme, slander* [1, 1, 34]
πτωχός, -ή, -όν, *poor* [4, 4, 34]
ὁμοίως, *likewise, in the same way* [1, 1, 31]
δείκνυμι, *I show, point out, make known* [2, 3, 30]
ἐπικαλέω, *I call (upon); I invoke* [1, 1, 30]
φίλος, -ου, ὁ, *loved, dear,* (subst.) *friend* [1, 2, 29]
πλούσιος, -α, -ον, *rich, wealthy* [2, 5, 28]
τελέω, *I finish, complete, fulfill* [1, 1, 28]
ἔλεος, -ους, τό, *pity, mercy, compassion* [2, 3, 27]
ἀδελφή, -ῆς, ἡ, *sister, fellow believer* [1, 1, 25]
θυσιαστήριον, -ου, τό, *altar, sanctuary* [1, 1, 23]
τελειόω, *I make perfect, complete, mature* [1, 1, 23]
ἐκλέγομαι, *I select, choose* [1, 1, 22]
Ἰσαάκ, ὁ, *Isaac* [1, 1, 20]
διακρίνω, *I discriminate, judge* [1, 3, 19]
κριτής, -ου, ὁ, *a judge* [1, 4, 19]
ἐλέγχω, *I convict, reprove* [1, 1, 18]
κενός, -ή, -όν, *empty, vain* [1, 1, 18]
πλησίον, *near,* (subst.) *a neighbor* [1, 2, 17]
ὦ, *oh!* [1, 1, 17]
τροφή, -ῆς, ἡ, *food* [1, 1, 16]
γυμνός, -ή, -όν, *naked* [1, 1, 15]
ἐπαγγέλλομαι, *I promise* [1, 2, 15]

κληρονόμος, -ου, ὁ, *an heir* [1, 1, 15]
μοιχεύω, *I commit adultery* [2, 2, 15]
χορτάζω, *I eat to the full, to be satisfied, be filled* [1, 1, 15]
διαλογισμός, -οῦ, ὁ, *a reasoning, questioning, thought* [1, 1, 14]
πόρνη, -ης, ἡ, *a prostitute* [1, 1, 12]
φονεύω, *I kill, murder* [2, 4, 12]
ἐλευθερία, -ας, ἡ, *liberty* [1, 2, 11]
ἀναφέρω, *I bring up, offer* [1, 1, 10]
ἔνοχος, -ον, *involved in, liable, guilty* [1, 1, 10]
λαμπρός, -ά, -όν, *bright* [2, 2, 9]
ἀργός, -ή, -όν, *inactive, idle* [1, 1, 8]
ἐσθής, -ῆτος, ἡ, *clothing* [3, 3, 8]
μέντοι, *yet, however* [1, 1, 8]
ἀτιμάζω, *I dishonor* [1, 1, 7]
ὑποπόδιον, -ου, τό, *a footstool* [1, 1, 7]
θερμαίνομαι, *I warm* [1, 1, 6]
λείπω, *I leave, leave behind, lack* [1, 3, 6]
φορέω, *I wear, bear* [1, 1, 6]
βασιλικός, -ή, -όν, *royal* [1, 1, 5]
παραβάτης, -ου, ὁ, *transgressor* [2, 2, 5]
πταίω, *I cause to stumble, I stumble* [1, 3, 5]
συνεργέω, *I work together* [1, 1, 5]
κατακαυχάομαι, *I exult over, triumph over* [1, 2, 4]
προσωπολημψία, -ας, ἡ, *respect of persons, partiality, personal favoritism* [1, 1, 4]
ὑποδέχομαι, *I welcome, receive, entertain as a guest* [1, 1, 4]
ἐπιβλέπω, *I look on (with favor), have regard for* [1, 1, 3]
κριτήριον, -ου, τό, *a law court, tribunal* [1, 1, 3]
ὄφελος, -ους, τό, *use, benefit, good* [2, 2, 3]
ἕλκω, *I drag* [1, 1, 2]
καταδυναστεύω, *I oppress* [1, 1, 2]
Ῥαάβ, ἡ, *Rahab* [1, 1, 2]
ῥυπαρός, -ά, -όν, *filthy, soiled* [1, 1, 2]
ἀνέλεος, -ον, *merciless* [1, 1, 1]
ἐπιτήδειος, -α, -ον, *necessary* [1, 1, 1]
ἐφήμερος, -ον, *daily* [1, 1, 1]
προσωπολημπτέω, *I show partiality* [1, 1, 1]

φρίσσω, *I shudder* [1, 1, 1]
χρυσοδακτύλιος, -ον, *with a gold ring* [1, 1, 1]

GRAMMATICAL OVERVIEW FOR JAMES 2

More frequently in this chapter than any other, you will encounter certain nouns (typically names) in a syntactical relationship known as "apposition." Essentially, a noun in apposition to another provides the reader with more information about the preceding noun (substantival participles can function in the same way). For example, in 2:21 it reads Ἀβραὰμ ὁ πατὴρ ἡμῶν. The nominative title (ὁ πατὴρ) is in apposition to Ἀβραὰμ. A translation reflects that the appositional noun is referring to Ἀβραὰμ when rendered "Abraham, our father."

Additionally, throughout this epistle, you will encounter many prepositional phrases in which the basic glosses memorized by beginning students is not appropriate given James's usage in the context of the passage. For example, in 2:18 the prepositional phrase ἐκ τῶν ἔργων μου should not be translated with the typical gloss "from" or "out of." Rather, given the context, it a prepositional phrase indicating means. Thus, a translation such as "by my faith" is preferable. In general, beginning readers of the Greek New Testament should be ready for prepositions to function in ways that may vary from your initial glosses committed to memory.

2.1 Ἀδελφοί μου, μὴ ἐν προσωπολημψίαις[1] ἔχετε τὴν
πίστιν τοῦ κυρίου[2] ἡμῶν Ἰησοῦ Χριστοῦ τῆς δόξης[3];
2 ἐὰν γὰρ εἰσέλθῃ[4] ⸀εἰς συναγωγὴν ὑμῶν ἀνὴρ
χρυσοδακτύλιος[5] ἐν ἐσθῆτι[6] λαμπρᾷ[7], εἰσέλθῃ δὲ καὶ
πτωχὸς[8] ἐν ῥυπαρᾷ[9] ἐσθῆτι[10], 3 ⸂ἐπιβλέψητε[11] δὲ⸃ ἐπὶ τὸν
φοροῦντα[12] τὴν ἐσθῆτα[13] τὴν λαμπρὰν[14] καὶ ⸀εἴπητε[15]·
Σὺ κάθου[16] ὧδε καλῶς[17], καὶ τῷ πτωχῷ[18] εἴπητε[19]·
Σὺ στῆθι[20] ⸂ἢ κάθου[21] ἐκεῖ⸃ ὑπὸ τὸ ὑποπόδιόν[22] μου,

---

[1] προσωπολημψία, -ας, ἡ, *respect of persons, partiality, personal favoritism.*
[2] TH: objective gen. *faith in our glorious Lord.*
[3] TH: Attrib. gen. modifying τοῦ κυρίου, *our glorious Lord.*
[4] MH: aor. act. subj. 3rd sg. from εἰσέρχομαι = pref. (εἰς) + root + 3rd sg. act. ending (εἰσ + ἐλθ + ῃ).
[5] χρυσοδακτύλιος, -ον, *with a gold ring.*
[6] ἐσθής, -ῆτος, ἡ, *clothing.*
[7] λαμπρός, -ά, -όν, *bright.*
[8] πτωχός, -ή, -όν, *poor.* TH: Used subst., *a poor person.*
[9] ῥυπαρός, -ά, -όν, *filthy, soiled.*
[10] ἐσθής, -ῆτος, ἡ, *clothing.*
[11] ἐπιβλέπω, *I look on (with favor), have regard for.* MH: aor. act. subj. 2nd pl. = pref. (ἐπί) + root + tense formative + lengthened connecting vowel + 2nd pl. act. ending (ἐπι + βλέπ + σ + η + τε). Review Square of Stops, π + σ › ψ.
[12] φορέω, *I wear, bear.* TH: pres. act. prtc. acc. masc. sg. used subst., *the one wearing.*
[13] ἐσθής, -ῆτος, ἡ, *clothing.*
[14] λαμπρός, -ά, -όν, *bright.*
[15] λέγω, *to say, speak.* MH: aor. act. subj. 2nd pl.
[16] TH: pres. mid./pass. impv. 2nd sg. from κάθημαι.
[17] καλῶς, *well, beautifully,* ***rightly***.
[18] πτωχός, -ή, -όν, *poor.*
[19] λέγω, *to say, speak.* TH: aor. act. subj. 2nd pl.
[20] TH: aor. act. impv. 2nd sg. from ἵστημι.
[21] TH: pres. mid./pass. impv. 2nd sg. from κάθημαι. NA[28] reads ἐκεῖ ἢ κάθου.
[22] ὑποπόδιον, -ου, τό, *a footstool.*

4 ⸂οὐ[1] διεκρίθητε[2] ἐν ἑαυτοῖς καὶ ἐγένεσθε κριταὶ[3]
διαλογισμῶν[4] πονηρῶν; **5** ἀκούσατε, ἀδελφοί μου
ἀγαπητοί. οὐχ ὁ θεὸς ἐξελέξατο[5] τοὺς πτωχοὺς[6] ⸀τῷ
κόσμῳ[7]⸁ πλουσίους[8] ἐν πίστει καὶ κληρονόμους[9] τῆς
βασιλείας[10] ἧς ἐπηγγείλατο[11] τοῖς ἀγαπῶσιν[12] αὐτόν;
6 ὑμεῖς δὲ ἠτιμάσατε[13] τὸν πτωχόν[14]. οὐχ οἱ πλούσιοι[15]
καταδυναστεύουσιν[16] ὑμῶν, καὶ αὐτοὶ ἕλκουσιν[17] ὑμᾶς εἰς

---

[1] NA[28] reads καί οὐ.

[2] διακρίνω, *I discriminate, judge*. MH: aor. pass. ind. 2nd pl. = pref. (διά) + aug. + root + tense formative + 2nd pl. pass. ending (δι + ε + κρί + θη + τε). The final vowel in the pref. (διά) is dropped due the verbal aug. (ε).

[3] κριτής, -ου, ὁ, *a judge*.

[4] διαλογισμός, -οῦ, ὁ, *a reasoning, questioning, thought*. TH: διαλογισμῶν πονηρῶν functioning as an attrib. gen., *judges with evil thoughts*.

[5] ἐκλέγομαι, *I select, choose*. MH: aor. mid. indic. 3rd sg. = pref. (ἐκ) + aug. + root + tense formative + 3rd sg. mid. ending (ἐξ + ε + λέγ + σα + το). Review Square of Stops, γ + σ › ξ. The κ in the pref. becomes ξ because of the vocalic verbal aug.

[6] πτωχός, -ή, -όν, *poor*, (subst. pl.) **the poor**.

[7] TH: Dative of reference/respect,*poor with respect to ("in the eyes of") the world.*

[8] πλούσιος, -α, -ον, *rich, wealthy*, (subst. pl.) **the rich.**

[9] κληρονόμος, -ου, ὁ, *an heir*.

[10] TH: Objective gen., the inheritance obtained by the heirs = the kingdom.

[11] ἐπαγγέλλομαι, *I promise*. MH: aor. mid. indic. 3rd sg. = pref. (ἐπί) + root (lengthened vowel as aug.) + tense formative + mid. 3rd sg. ending (ἐπ + ηγγείλ + α + το). Verbs with a root beg. with a vowel will take a lengthened vowel as the aug. (α › η). Aor. tense formative (σα) drops the σ in a liquid verb (λ, μ, ν, or ρ).

[12] TH: pres. act. prtc. dat. masc. pl. from ἀγαπάω. Subst. prtc., *those who love*.

[13] ἀτιμάζω, *I dishonor*. MH: aor. act. indic. 2nd pl. = root (lengthened vowel as aug.) + tense formative + act. 2nd pl. ending (ἠτιμά + σα + τε). Verbs with a root beg. with a vowel will take a lengthened vowel as the aug. (α › η).

[14] πτωχός, -ή, -όν, *poor*, (subst. sg.) **the poor man.**

[15] πλούσιος, -α, -ον, *rich, wealthy*, (subst. pl.) **the rich.**

[16] καταδυναστεύω, *I oppress*.

[17] ἕλκω, *I drag*.

κριτήρια[1]; **7** οὐκ αὐτοὶ[2] βλασφημοῦσιν[3] τὸ καλὸν ὄνομα τὸ[4]
ἐπικληθὲν[5] ἐφ᾽ ὑμᾶς[6];

8 Εἰ μέντοι[7] νόμον τελεῖτε[8] βασιλικὸν[9] κατὰ τὴν
γραφήν Ἀγαπήσεις[10] τὸν πλησίον[11] σου ὡς σεαυτόν[12],
καλῶς[13] ποιεῖτε· **9** εἰ δὲ προσωπολημπτεῖτε[14], ἁμαρτίαν
ἐργάζεσθε[15], ἐλεγχόμενοι[16] ὑπὸ τοῦ νόμου ὡς παραβάται[17].
10 ὅστις γὰρ ὅλον[18] τὸν νόμον τηρήσῃ[19], πταίσῃ[20] δὲ ἐν ἑνί[21],

---

[1] κριτήριον, -ου, τό, *a law court, tribunal.*

[2] TH: Intensive pron., *they themselves.*

[3] βλασφημέω, *I revile sacred things, slander,* ***I blaspheme****.*

[4] TH: Common function of the art. is usage as rel. pron., *that, which.*

[5] ἐπικαλέω, *I call (upon); I invoke.* MH: aor. pass. prtc. acc. masc. pl. from ἐπικαλέω = pref. (ἐπί) + root + tense formative + pass. prtc. morpheme (ἐπι + κλη + θὲ + ν). The -τ drops off of the -ντ pass. prtc. morpheme because it is ending the prtc., has no case ending.

[6] TH: τὸ ἐπικληθὲν ἐφ᾽ ὑμᾶς = rel. pron. + pass. prtc. + ἐπί + acc. = *that was called over you.*

[7] μέντοι, *yet, however.*

[8] τελέω, *I finish, complete, fulfill.*

[9] βασιλικός, -ή, -όν, *royal.*

[10] TH: fut. act. indic. 2nd sg. from ἀγαπάω. Fut. force of impv., *you shall love.*

[11] πλησίον, *near, (subst.)* ***a neighbor****.*

[12] σεαυτοῦ, -ῆς, *of yourself.*

[13] καλῶς, *well, beautifully.*

[14] προσωπολημπτέω, *I show partiality.*

[15] ἐργάζομαι, *I work, perform, accomplish.*

[16] ἐλέγχω, *I convict, reprove.* TH: pres. pass. prtc. nom. masc. pl. Adverbial prtc. of result, *resulting in being convicted.*

[17] παραβάτης, -ου, ὁ, *transgressor.*

[18] TH: ὅλον functions as an attrib. adj. to τὸν νόμον, *the whole law.*

[19] TH: aor. act. subj. 3rd sg. from τηρέω.

[20] πταίω, *I cause to stumble, I stumble.* TH: aor. act. subj. 3rd sg.

[21] TH: dat. masc./neut. sg. from εἷς, *one thing.*

γέγονεν πάντων[1] ἔνοχος[2]. **11** ὁ γὰρ εἰπών[3]· Μὴ ⸀μοιχεύσῃς[4]
εἶπεν[5] καί· Μὴ ⸀φονεύσῃς[6]· εἰ δὲ οὐ ⸂μοιχεύεις[7] φονεύεις[8]⸃
δέ, γέγονας παραβάτης[9] νόμου. **12** οὕτως λαλεῖτε[10] καὶ
οὕτως ποιεῖτε[11] ὡς διὰ[12] νόμου ἐλευθερίας[13] μέλλοντες[14]
κρίνεσθαι[15]. **13** ἡ γὰρ κρίσις[16] ἀνέλεος[17] τῷ μὴ ποιήσαντι[18]
ἔλεος[19]· κατακαυχᾶται[20] ⸀ἔλεος[21] κρίσεως[22].

---

1 TH: ἔνοχος with gen. complement denotes per. or thing sinned against, *guilty of all.*

2 ἔνοχος, -ον, *involved in, liable, guilty.* TH: pred. adj. of γέγονεν.

3 λέγω, *to say, speak.* TH: subst. prtc., *he who said.*

4 μοιχεύω, *I commit adultery.* TH: Prohibitive subj., *do not commit adultery.*

5 λέγω, *to say, speak.*

6 φονεύω, *I kill, murder.* TH: Prohibitive subj., *do not murder.*

7 μοιχεύω, *I commit adultery.*

8 φονεύω, *I kill, murder.*

9 παραβάτης, -ου, ὁ, *transgressor.* TH: Pred. nom. of γέγονας.

10 TH: pres. act. impv. 2nd pl. from λαλέω.

11 TH: pres. act. impv. 2nd pl. from ποιέω.

12 TH: διά + gen., *by (means of).*

13 ἐλευθερία, -ας, ἡ, *liberty.*

14 TH: pres. act. prtc. nom. masc. pl. from μέλλω. Subst. prtc., *those who are about to.*

15 TH: pres. pass. inf. from κρίνω. Complementary inf. completing μέλλοντες, *those who are about to be judged.*

16 κρίσις, -εως, ἡ, *judging, trial, judgment.* TH: Subject nominative of implied verb.

17 ἀνέλεος, -ον, *merciless.* TH: Pred. adj. of implied verb.

18 TH: aor. act. prtc. dat. masc. sg. from ποιέω. Subst. prtc., *to one who does not do mercy.*

19 ἔλεος, -ους, τό, *pity, mercy, compassion.*

20 κατακαυχάομαι, *I exult over, triumph over.*

21 ἔλεος, -ους, τό, *pity, mercy, compassion.*

22 κρίσις, -εως, ἡ, *judging, trial, judgment.* TH: Gen. obj. of κατακαυχᾶται.

14 ⸀Τί ὄφελος[1], ἀδελφοί μου, ἐὰν πίστιν λέγῃ τις[2] ἔχειν[3]
ἔργα δὲ μὴ ἔχῃ; μὴ δύναται ἡ[4] πίστις σῶσαι[5] αὐτόν; **15** ⸀ἐὰν
ἀδελφὸς ἢ ἀδελφὴ[6] γυμνοὶ[7] ὑπάρχωσιν καὶ ⸀λειπόμενοι[8]
τῆς ἐφημέρου[9] τροφῆς[10], **16** εἴπῃ[11] δέ τις αὐτοῖς ἐξ ὑμῶν[12]·
Ὑπάγετε[13] ἐν εἰρήνῃ, θερμαίνεσθε[14] καὶ χορτάζεσθε[15], μὴ
δῶτε[16] δὲ αὐτοῖς τὰ ἐπιτήδεια[17] τοῦ σώματος, ⸀τί ὄφελος[18];
17 οὕτως καὶ ἡ πίστις, ἐὰν μὴ ⸂ἔχῃ ἔργα⸃, νεκρά ἐστιν[19]
καθ᾽ ἑαυτήν[20].

---

[1] ὄφελος, -ους, τό, *use, benefit, good.*
[2] TH: Subject of subj. verb, λέγῃ.
[3] TH: pres. act. inf. from ἔχω. Inf. of indir. discourse, *if someone says he has faith.*
[4] TH: Anaphoric art., *such a faith, that faith* (referring to the faith previously described in v. 14).
[5] TH: aor. act. inf. from σῴζω. Complementary inf. of δύναται, *able to save.*
[6] ἀδελφή, -ῆς, ἡ, *sister, fellow believer.*
[7] γυμνός, -ή, -όν, *naked.*
[8] λείπω, *I leave, leave behind, lack.* NA[28] adds ὦσιν after λειπόμενοι.
[9] ἐφήμερος, -ον, *daily.*
[10] τροφή, -ῆς, ἡ, *food.* TH: τῆς ἐφημέρου τροφῆς, gen. obj. of λειπόμενοι.
[11] λέγω, *to say, speak.* MH: aor. act. subj. 3rd sg. = second aor. root + 3rd sg. act. ending (εἴπ + ῃ).
[12] TH: τις…ἐξ ὑμῶν, *one of you.*
[13] TH: pres. act. impv. 2nd pl. from ὑπαγω.
[14] θερμαίνομαι, *I warm.* MH: pres. mid. impv. 2nd pl. from θερμαίνομαι = root + connecting vowel + 2nd pl. mid. ending (θερμαίν + ε + σθε).
[15] χορτάζω, *I eat to the full, to be satisfied, be filled.* MH: pres. pass. impv. 2nd pl. = root + connecting vowel + 2nd pl. mid. ending (χορτάζ + ε + σθε).
[16] TH: aor. act. subj. 2nd pl. from δίδωμι.
[17] ἐπιτήδειος, -α, -ον, *necessary.* TH: Function subst., *the necessary things, necessities.*
[18] ὄφελος, -ους, τό, *use, benefit, good.* NA has τί τὸ ὄφελος.
[19] TH: The subject of ἐστιν is ἡ πίστις.
[20] TH: prep. phrase καθ᾽ ἑαυτήν, *by itself.*

18 Ἀλλ᾽ ἐρεῖ[1] τις· Σὺ πίστιν ἔχεις κἀγὼ ἔργα ἔχω[2].
δεῖξόν[3] μοι τὴν πίστιν σου ⸀χωρὶς[4] τῶν ⸀ἔργων, κἀγώ ⸂σοι
δείξω[5]⸃ ἐκ[6] τῶν ἔργων μου τὴν ⸀πίστιν. **19** σὺ πιστεύεις ὅτι
⸂εἷς[7] ἐστιν ὁ θεός[8]⸃; καλῶς[9] ποιεῖς· καὶ τὰ δαιμόνια
πιστεύουσιν καὶ φρίσσουσιν[10]. **20** θέλεις δὲ γνῶναι[11], ὦ[12]
ἄνθρωπε κενέ[13], ὅτι ἡ πίστις χωρὶς[14] τῶν ἔργων ⸀ἀργή[15]
ἐστιν; **21** Ἀβραὰμ ὁ πατὴρ[16] ἡμῶν οὐκ[17] ἐξ[18] ἔργων

---

[1] λέγω, *to say, speak.* MH: fut. act. indic. 3rd sg. = root + connecting vowel + 3rd sg. act. ending (ἐρ + ε + ῖ).

[2] TH: The end of the opponent's interlocution is unclear. Likely, δεῖξόν begins James's response.

[3] δείκνυμι, *I show, point out, make known.* MH: aor. act. impv. 2nd sg. = root + tense formative + 2nd sg. act. ending (δεῖκ + σ + όν). Review Square of Stops, k + σ › ξ.

[4] χωρίς, (gen.) *without, apart from.*

[5] δείκνυμι, *I show, point out, make known.* MH: fut. act. indic. 1st sg. = root + tense formative + 1st sg. act. ending (δείκ + σ + ω). Review Square of Stops, k + σ › ξ.

[6] TH: Prep. of means, *by (means of).*

[7] TH: Pred. adj. of ἐστιν.

[8] TH: Nom. subject of ἐστιν.

[9] καλῶς, *well, beautifully.*

[10] φρίσσω, *I shudder.*

[11] TH: aor. act. inf. from γινώσκω. Complementary inf. of θέλεις, *do you want to understand?*

[12] ὦ, *oh!*

[13] κενός, -ή, -όν, *empty, vain.*

[14] χωρίς, (gen.) *without, apart from.*

[15] ἀργός, -ή, -όν, *inactive, idle.*

[16] TH: Nom. of app. to Ἀβραάμ.

[17] TH: Indicates a question expecting a positive answer.

[18] TH: Prep. of means, *by (means of).*

ἐδικαιώθη[1], ἀνενέγκας[2] Ἰσαὰκ[3] τὸν υἱὸν[4] αὐτοῦ ἐπὶ τὸ
θυσιαστήριον[5]; **22** βλέπεις ὅτι ἡ πίστις συνήργει[6] τοῖς
ἔργοις αὐτοῦ καὶ ἐκ[7] τῶν ἔργων ἡ πίστις ἐτελειώθη[8],
23 καὶ ἐπληρώθη ἡ γραφὴ ἡ λέγουσα[9]· Ἐπίστευσεν δὲ
Ἀβραὰμ τῷ θεῷ[10], καὶ ἐλογίσθη[11] αὐτῷ εἰς δικαιοσύνην,
καὶ φίλος[12] θεοῦ ἐκλήθη[13]. **24** ὁρᾶτε[14] ὅτι ἐξ[15] ἔργων
δικαιοῦται[16] ἄνθρωπος καὶ οὐκ ἐκ[17] πίστεως μόνον.

---

[1] δικαιόω, *I set right, I justify, **to consider righteous***. MH: aor. pass. indic. 3rd sg. = aug. + root + tense formative (ἐ + δικαιώ + θη + ε). There is technically no 3rd sg. aor. pass. per. ending, the tense formative ends the verb.

[2] ἀναφέρω, *I bring up, offer*. TH: aor. act. prtc. nom. masc. sg. Temporal prtc., *after he offered.* Possibly causal prtc., *because he offered.*

[3] Ἰσαάκ, ὁ, *Isaac.*

[4] TH: Acc. of app. to Ἰσαάκ.

[5] θυσιαστήριον, -ου, τό, *altar, sanctuary.*

[6] συνεργέω, *I work together*. MH: impf. act. indic. 3rd sg. = pref. (σύν) + aug. + root + connecting vowel + 3rd sg. act. ending (συν + ήργ + ε + ι). Aug. lengthens vowel beg. the root.

[7] TH: Prep. of means, *by (means of).*

[8] τελειόω, *I make perfect, complete, mature*. MH: aor. pass. indic. 3rd sg. = aug. + root + tense formative (ἐ + τελειώ + θη). There is technically no 3rd sg. aor. pass. per. ending, the tense formative ends the verb.

[9] TH: pres. act. prtc. nom. fem. sg. from λέγω. Attrib. adj. prtc., *the Scripture which says.*

[10] TH: πιστεύω + dat. dir. obj. = *gives credence to, believes.*

[11] λογίζομαι, *I reckon, consider, think, count.*

[12] φίλος, -ου, ὁ, *loved, dear,* (subst.) ***friend***.

[13] MH: aor. pass. indic. 3rd sg. from καλέω = aug. + root + tense formative (ἐ + κλή + θη). There is technically no 3rd sg. aor. pass. per. ending, the tense formative ends the verb.

[14] TH: Pres. act. indic. 2nd pl. from ὁράω.

[15] TH: Prep. of means, *by (means of).*

[16] δικαιόω, *I set right, I justify, **to consider righteous**.*

[17] TH: Prep. of means, *by (means of).*

25 ὁμοίως[1] δὲ καὶ Ῥαὰβ[2] ἡ πόρνη[3] οὐκ ἐξ[4] ἔργων
ἐδικαιώθη[5], ὑποδεξαμένη[6] τοὺς ἀγγέλους καὶ ἑτέρᾳ ὁδῷ
ἐκβαλοῦσα[7]; **26** ὥσπερ[8] ⸀γὰρ[9] τὸ σῶμα[10] χωρὶς[11] πνεύματος
νεκρόν[12] ἐστιν, οὕτως καὶ ἡ πίστις[13] ⸀χωρὶς[14] ἔργων νεκρά[15]
ἐστιν.

---

[1] ὁμοίως, *likewise, in the same way.*
[2] Ῥαάβ, ἡ, *Rahab.*
[3] πόρνη, -ης, ἡ, *a prostitute.* TH: Nom. of app. to Ῥαὰβ.
[4] TH: Prep. of means, *by (means of).*
[5] δικαιόω, *I set right, I justify,* ***to consider righteous.***
[6] ὑποδέχομαι, *I welcome, receive, entertain as a guest.* TH: aor. mid. prtc. nom. fem. sg. Temporal prtc., *after she received the messengers.* Possibly causal prtc., *because she received the messengers.*
[7] TH: aor. act. prtc. nom. fem. sg. from ἐκβάλλω. Temporal prtc., *after she sent out.* Possibly causal prtc., *because she sent out.*
[8] ὥσπερ, *just as* (more emphatic than ὡς).
[9] TH: Explanatory γάρ. What follows is supporting explanation of a prec. argument.
[10] TH: Nom. subject of ἐστιν.
[11] χωρίς, (gen.) *without, apart from.*
[12] TH: Pred. adj. of ἐστιν.
[13] TH: Nom. subject of ἐστιν.
[14] χωρίς, (gen.) *without, apart from.*
[15] TH: Pred. adj. of ἐστιν.

SBLGNT SIGLA APPARATUS FOR JAMES 2

ˀ **2:2 εἰς** WH Treg NA28] + τὴν RP
ˁ **3 ἐπιβλέψητε δὲ** WH NA28] καὶ ἐπιβλέψητε Treg RP
ˋ **3 ἐπιβλέψητε δὲ** WH NA28] καὶ ἐπιβλέψητε Treg RP

ˀ • **εἴπητε** WH Treg NA28] + αὐτῷ RP

ˁ • **ἢ κάθου ἐκεῖ** WH NA28] ἐκεῖ ἢ κάθου Treg NA27; ἐκεῖ ἢ κάθου ὧδε RP

ˋ • **ἢ κάθου ἐκεῖ** WH NA28] ἐκεῖ ἢ κάθου Treg NA27; ἐκεῖ ἢ κάθου ὧδε RP

ˀ **4 οὐ** WH Treg NA27] καὶ οὐ NA28 RP
ˁ **5 τῷ κόσμῳ** WH Treg NA28] τοῦ κόσμου RP
ˋ **5 τῷ κόσμῳ** WH Treg NA28] τοῦ κόσμου RP
ˁ **10 τηρήσῃ πταίσῃ** WH Treg NA28] τηρήσει πταίσει RP
ˋ **10 τηρήσῃ πταίσῃ** WH Treg NA28] τηρήσει πταίσει RP
ˀ **11 μοιχεύσῃς** WH Treg NA28] μοιχεύσεις RP

ˀ • **φονεύσῃς** WH Treg NA28] φονεύσεις RP

ˁ • **μοιχεύεις φονεύεις** WH Treg NA28] μοιχεύσεις φονεύσεις RP

ˋ • **μοιχεύεις φονεύεις** WH Treg NA28] μοιχεύσεις φονεύσεις RP

ˀ **13 ἔλεος** WH Treg NA28] ἔλεον RP
ˀ **14 Τί** WH] + τὸ Treg NA28 RP
ˀ **15 ἐὰν** WH Treg NA28] + δὲ RP

ˀ • **λειπόμενοι** WH Treg NA27] + ὦσιν NA28 RP

ˀ **16 τί** WH] + τὸ Treg NA28 RP
ˁ **17 ἔχῃ ἔργα** WH Treg NA28] ἔργα ἔχῃ RP
ˋ **17 ἔχῃ ἔργα** WH Treg NA28] ἔργα ἔχῃ RP
ˀ **18 χωρὶς** WH Treg NA28] ἐκ RP

ˀ • **ἔργων** WH Treg NA28] + σου RP

ˁ • **σοι δείξω** WH Treg NA28] δείξω σοι RP

ˋ • **σοι δείξω** WH Treg NA28] δείξω σοι RP

ˀ • **πίστιν** WH Treg NA28] + μου RP

ˁ **19 εἷς ἐστιν ὁ θεός** Treg NA28] εἷς θεός ἐστιν WH; ὁ θεὸς εἷς ἐστιν RP
ˋ **19 εἷς ἐστιν ὁ θεός** Treg NA28] εἷς θεός ἐστιν WH; ὁ θεὸς εἷς ἐστιν RP
ˀ **20 ἀργή** WH Treg NA28] νεκρά RP
ˀ **24 ὁρᾶτε** WH Treg NA28] + τοίνυν RP
ˀ **26 γὰρ** Treg NA28 RP] – WH

ˀ • **χωρὶς** WH NA28] + τῶν Treg RP

JAMES 3

NEW VOCABULARY BY FREQUENCY

[Chapter, Book, SBLGNT Occurrences]

θηρίον, -ου, τό, *wild beast* [1, 1, 46]
μικρός, -ά, -όν, *small, little* [1, 1, 46]
εὐλογέω, *I speak well of, praise, bless* [1, 1, 41]
βούλομαι, *I wish, I intend* [1, 3, 37]
ἅπας, -ασα, -αν, *all, every, whole* [1, 1, 34]
μέλος, -ους, τό, *limb, member, (body) part* [2, 3, 34]
δυνατός, -ή, -όν, *powerful, able, capable* [1, 1, 32]
ἄνεμος, -ου, ὁ, *wind* [1, 1, 31]
δείκνυμι, *I show, point out, make known* [1, 3, 30]
ἀδικία, -ας, ἡ, *wrongdoing, injustice, unrighteousness* [1, 1, 25]
ἔλεος, -ους, τό, *pity, mercy, compassion* [1, 3, 27]
κρίμα, -τος, τό, *decision, judgment, condemnation* [1, 1, 27]
καθίστημι, *I set down, I set in order, appoint* [1, 2, 21]
σοφός, -ή, -όν, *skillful, wise* [1, 1, 19]
ἵππος, -ου, ὁ, *a horse* [1, 1, 17]
ἔπειτα, *then* [1, 2, 16]
εὐλογία, -ας, ἡ, *a blessing* [1, 1, 16]
ζῆλος, -ου, ὁ, *zeal, jealousy* [2, 2, 16]
συκῆ, -ῆς, ἡ, *a fig tree* [1, 1, 16]
ἐλαία, -ας, ἡ, *an olive tree* [1, 1, 15]
κατέρχομαι, *I come down, go down* [1, 1, 15]
ἐλάχιστος, *very small* [1, 1, 14]
πετεινόν, -ου, τό, *a bird* [1, 1, 14]
φύσις, -εως, ἡ, *nature* [2, 2, 14]
ἀναστροφή, -ῆς, ἡ, *conduct* [1, 1, 13]
ἄνωθεν, *from above, again* [2, 3, 13]
γέεννα, -ης, ἡ, *Gehenna* [1, 1, 12]
ψεύδομαι, *I lie* [1, 1, 12]
πηγή, -ῆς, ἡ, *a spring, fountain* [1, 1, 11]
πρᾶγμα, -τος, τό, *a deed, matter, thing* [1, 1, 11]
πραΰτης, -ητος, ἡ, *gentleness, humility, courtesy* [1, 2, 11]

ἄμπελος, -ου, ἡ, *vine* [1, 1, 9]
μεστός, -ή, -όν, *full* [2, 2, 9]
ἁγνός, -ή, -όν, *pure, holy, chaste, innocent* [1, 1, 8]
ἀνθρώπινος, -η, -ον, *human* [1, 1, 7]
ἐπίγειος, -ον, *of the earth, earthly* [1, 1, 7]
ἐριθεία, -ας, ἡ, *rivalry, ambition* [2, 2, 7]
ἀνυπόκριτος, -ον, *sincere, without hypocrisy, genuine* [1, 1, 6]
κατάρα, -ας, ἡ, *a curse* [1, 1, 6]
φαῦλος, -η, -ον, *worthless, bad* [1, 1, 6]
ψυχικός, -ή, -όν, *natural, wordly-minded* [1, 1, 6]
ἀκαταστασία, -ας, ἡ, *a disturbance, disorder, tumult* [1, 1, 5]
γένεσις, -εως, ἡ, *origin, birth, genealogy* [1, 2, 5]
ἐλαύνω, *I drive or push, I row* [1, 1, 5]
ἐπιεικής, -ές, *yielding, gentle, kind, courteous* [1, 1, 5]
καταράομαι, *I curse* [1, 1, 5]
πταίω, *I cause to stumble, I stumble* [2, 3, 5]
σκληρός, -ά, -όν, *hard, rough, strong* [1, 1, 5]
γλυκύς, -εια, -ύ, *sweet* [2, 2, 4]
δαμάζω, *I tame, subdue* [3, 3, 4]
ἑρπετόν, -οῦ, τό, *a creeping thing, reptile* [1, 1, 4]
κατακαυχάομαι, *I exult over, triumph over* [1, 2, 4]
τηλικοῦτος, -αύτη, -οῦτο, *so great, so large* [1, 1, 4]
ἡλίκος, -η, -ον, *how great, how small* [2, 2, 3]
ἰός, -οῦ, ὁ, *rust, poison* [1, 2, 3]
ἀκατάστατος, -ον, *unstable, restless* [1, 2, 2]
ἀνάπτω, *I kindle* [1, 1, 2]
εἰρηνικός, -ή, -όν, *peaceable, peaceful* [1, 1, 2]
εὐθύνω, *I make straight; I guide straight* [1, 1, 2]
μετάγω, *I guide, direct* [2, 2, 2]
ὁρμή, -ῆς, ἡ, *impulse, inclination, attempt* [1, 1, 2]
πηδάλιον, -ου, τό, *a rudder* [1, 1, 2]
πικρός, -ά, -όν, *bitter* [2, 2, 2]
ὀπή, -ῆς, ἡ, *opening, hole* [1, 1, 2]
σπιλόω, *I stain, defile, pollute* [1, 1, 2]
φλογίζω, *I set on fire* [2, 2, 2]
χαλινός, -οῦ, ὁ, *a bit, bridle* [1, 1, 2]
ἀδιάκριτος, -ον, *unwavering* [1, 1, 1]

ἁλυκός, -ή, -όν, *salty* [1, 1, 1]
αὐχέω, *I boast* [1, 1, 1]
βρύω, *I pour forth* [1, 1, 1]
δαιμονιώδης, -ες, *demonic, devilish* [1, 1, 1]
ἐνάλιος, *belonging to the sea, marine creatures* [1, 1, 1]
ἐπιστήμων, -ον, *expert, skilled, understanding* [1, 1, 1]
εὐπειθής, -ές, *compliant, obedient* [1, 1, 1]
θανατηφόρος, -ον, *death-bringing, deadly* [1, 1, 1]
ὁμοίωσις, -εως, ἡ, *a likeness, resemblance* [1, 1, 1]
ὕλη, -ης, ἡ, *a forest, wood, timber* [1, 1, 1]
χρή, *it is necessary, it ought* [1, 1, 1]

3.1 Μὴ πολλοὶ[1] διδάσκαλοι γίνεσθε[2], ἀδελφοί μου, εἰδότες[3] ὅτι μεῖζον κρίμα[4] λημψόμεθα[5]· **2** πολλὰ γὰρ πταίομεν[6] ἅπαντες[7]. εἴ τις ἐν λόγῳ οὐ πταίει[8], οὗτος τέλειος[9] ἀνήρ, δυνατὸς[10] χαλιναγωγῆσαι[11] καὶ ὅλον τὸ σῶμα. **3** ⸀εἰ δὲ⸌ τῶν ἵππων[12] τοὺς χαλινοὺς[13] εἰς τὰ στόματα βάλλομεν ⸂εἰς τὸ πείθεσθαι[14] αὐτοὺς ἡμῖν, καὶ ὅλον τὸ σῶμα αὐτῶν μετάγομεν[15]. **4** ἰδοὺ καὶ τὰ πλοῖα, τηλικαῦτα[16] ὄντα[17] καὶ ὑπὸ ⸂ἀνέμων[18] σκληρῶν[19]⸃ ἐλαυνόμενα[20],

---

[1] TH: Nom. subject of γίνεσθε, *not many (of you).*
[2] TH: Pres. mid./pass. impv. 2nd pl. from γίνομαι. Μή + impv. is a prohibition.
[3] MH: pf. act. prtc. nom. masc. pl. from οἶδα = root + prtc. morpheme + nom. masc. pl. ending (εἰδ + ότ + ες). TH: Causal prtc., *because you know.*
[4] κρίμα, -τος, τό, *decision, judgment, condemnation.*
[5] MH: fut. mid. indic. 1st pl. from λαμβάνω = root + tense formative + connecting vowel + 1st sg. mid./pass. ending (λημβ + σ + ο + μεθα). Review Square of Stops, β + σ › ψ.
[6] πταίω, *I cause to stumble, I stumble.*
[7] ἅπας, -ασα, -αν, *all, every, whole.* TH: Adj. modifying the implied subject of πταίομεν, *we all stumble.*
[8] πταίω, *I cause to stumble, I stumble.*
[9] τέλειος, -α, -ον, *perfect, complete, mature.*
[10] δυνατός, -ή, -όν, *powerful, able, capable.* TH: Nom. of app. to τέλειος ἀνήρ.
[11] χαλιναγωγέω, *I bridle, hold in check.* TH: aor. act. inf. Complementary inf. completing δυνατός, *able to bridle.*
[12] ἵππος, -ου, ὁ, *a horse.*
[13] χαλινός, -οῦ, ὁ, *a bit, bridle.*
[14] TH: εἰς + articular inf. indicates purpose. Inf. often takes acc. subject, εἰς τὸ πείθεσθαι αὐτοὺς. *In order that they obey.*
[15] μετάγω, *I guide, direct.*
[16] τηλικοῦτος, -αύτη, -οῦτο, *so great, so large.* TH: Pred. nom. of ὄντα.
[17] TH: pres. act. prtc. nom. neut. pl. from εἰμί. Concessive prtc., *although being.*
[18] ἄνεμος, -ου, ὁ, *wind.*
[19] σκληρός, -ά, -όν, *hard, rough, strong.*
[20] ἐλαύνω, *I drive or push, I row.* TH: pres. pass. prtc. nom. neut. pl. Concessive prtc., *although driven.*

μετάγεται[1] ὑπὸ ἐλαχίστου[2] πηδαλίου[3] ὅπου ⸂ἡ ὁρμὴ[4] τοῦ
εὐθύνοντος[5] βούλεται[6]⸃· **5** οὕτως καὶ ἡ γλῶσσα μικρὸν[7]
μέλος[8] ἐστὶν καὶ ⸂μεγάλα αὐχεῖ[9]⸃.

Ἰδοὺ ⸀ἡλίκον[10] πῦρ ἡλίκην[11] ὕλην[12] ἀνάπτει[13]· **6** καὶ
ἡ γλῶσσα πῦρ[14], ὁ κόσμος[15] τῆς ⸀ἀδικίας[16] ἡ γλῶσσα
καθίσταται[17] ἐν τοῖς μέλεσιν[18] ἡμῶν, ἡ σπιλοῦσα[19] ὅλον
τὸ σῶμα καὶ φλογίζουσα[20] τὸν τροχὸν[21] τῆς γενέσεως[22] καὶ

---

[1] μετάγω, *I guide, direct.*
[2] ἐλάχιστος, *very small.*
[3] πηδάλιον, -ου, τό, *a rudder.*
[4] ὁρμή, -ῆς, ἡ, *impulse, inclination, attempt.* TH: Subject of βούλεται.
[5] εὐθύνω, *I make straight.* TH: pres. act. prtc. gen. masc. sg. Subst. prtc., *the one who makes straight, the pilot.*
[6] βούλομαι, *I wish, I intend.*
[7] μικρός, -ά, -όν, *small, little.*
[8] μέλος, -ους, τό, *limb, member,* ***(body) part.***
[9] αὐχέω, *I boast.*
[10] ἡλίκος, -η, -ον, *how great,* ***how small.*** TH: ἡλίκον πῦρ subject of ἀνάπτει.
[11] ἡλίκος, -η, -ον, *how small,* ***how great.***
[12] ὕλη, -ης, ἡ, *a forest, wood, timber.*
[13] ἀνάπτω, *I kindle.*
[14] TH: Ἡ γλῶσσα, nom. subject in a verbless clause. Πῦρ, pred. nom. in a verbless clause, *the tongue is a fire.*
[15] TH: Nom. complement to ἡ γλῶσσα.
[16] ἀδικία, -ας, ἡ, *wrongdoing, injustice, unrighteousness.* TH: Gen. of content, *world full of unrighteousness.* Or, attrib. gen., *unrighteous world.*
[17] καθίστημι, *I set down, I set in order, appoint.* MH: pres. pass. indic. 3rd sg. = pref. (κατά) + root + shortened stem vowel (η › α) + pass. 3rd sg. ending (καθ + ίστ + α + ται); κατά followed by a rough breathing goes to καθ'.
[18] μέλος, -ους, τό, *limb, member, (body) part.*
[19] σπιλόω, *I stain, defile, pollute.* TH: pres. act. prtc. nom. fem. sg. Attribut. prtc. modifying ἡ γλῶσσα, *which stains.*
[20] φλογίζω, *I set on fire.* TH: pres. act. prtc. nom. fem. sg. Attribut. prtc. modifying ἡ γλῶσσα, *which sets on fire.*
[21] τροχός, -οῦ, ὁ, *a wheel, course.*
[22] γένεσις, -εως, ἡ, *origin, birth, genealogy,* ***life.*** TH: the phrase τὸν τροχὸν τῆς

φλογιζομένη[1] ὑπὸ τῆς γεέννης[2]. 7 πᾶσα γὰρ φύσις[3] θηρίων[4]
τε καὶ[5] πετεινῶν[6] ἑρπετῶν[7] τε καὶ ἐναλίων[8] δαμάζεται[9]
καὶ δεδάμασται[10] τῇ φύσει[11] τῇ ἀνθρωπίνῃ[12]· 8 τὴν δὲ
γλῶσσαν οὐδεὶς ⸂δαμάσαι[13] δύναται ἀνθρώπων[14]⸃·
⸀ἀκατάστατον[15] κακόν, μεστὴ[16] ἰοῦ[17] θανατηφόρου[18].
9 ἐν αὐτῇ[19] εὐλογοῦμεν[20] τὸν ⸀κύριον καὶ πατέρα, καὶ ἐν
αὐτῇ καταρώμεθα[21] τοὺς ἀνθρώπους τοὺς[22] καθ᾿ ὁμοίωσιν[23]

γενέσεως, lit. *wheel of becoming*, perhps *course of life.*

[1] φλογίζω, *I set on fire.* TH: pres. pass. prtc. nom. fem. sg. from φλογίζω. Attribut. prtc. modifying ἡ γλῶσσα, *which is set on fire.*

[2] γέεννα, -ης, ἡ, *Gehenna.*

[3] φύσις, -εως, ἡ, *nature, kind,* ***species.***

[4] θηρίον, -ου, τό, *wild beast.*

[5] TH: τε καὶ, *both...and.*

[6] πετεινόν, -ου, τό, *a bird.*

[7] ἑρπετόν, -οῦ, τό, *a creeping thing, reptile.*

[8] ἐνάλιος, *belonging to the sea, marine creatures.*

[9] δαμάζω, *I tame, subdue.*

[10] δαμάζω, *I tame, subdue.*

[11] φύσις, -εως, ἡ, *nature, kind,* ***species.***

[12] ἀνθρώπινος, -η, -ον, *human.* TH: τῇ φύσει τῇ ἀνθρωπίνῃ, dative of agency, *by the human*

[13] δαμάζω, *I tame, subdue.* TH: aor. act. inf. from δαμάζω. Complementary infinitive completing δύναται, *able to tame.*

[14] TH: Poss. gen., *tame the tongue of human beings.* Or, partitive gen., *no one of human beings is able.*

[15] ἀκατάστατος, -ον, *unstable, restless.* TH: ἀκατάστατον κακόν, where ἀκατάστατον functions attrib. and κακόν functions subst., *restless evil.*

[16] μεστός, -ή, -όν, *full.*

[17] ἰός, -οῦ, ὁ, *rust, poison.* TH: Gen. of content, *full of deadly poison.*

[18] θανατηφόρος, -ον, *death-bringing.* TH: Gen. of content, *full of deadly poison.*

[19] TH: Ante. = τὴν γλῶσσαν.

[20] εὐλογέω, *I speak well of, praise, bless.*

[21] καταράομαι, *I curse.*

[22] TH: Common function of the art. is usage as rel. pron., *that, which, who.*

[23] ὁμοίωσις, -εως, ἡ, *a likeness, resemblance.*

θεοῦ γεγονότας[1]· **10** ἐκ τοῦ αὐτοῦ στόματος ἐξέρχεται
εὐλογία[2] καὶ κατάρα[3]. οὐ χρή[4], ἀδελφοί μου, ταῦτα[5] οὕτως
γίνεσθαι[6]. **11** μήτι[7] ἡ πηγὴ[8] ἐκ τῆς αὐτῆς ὀπῆς[9] βρύει[10] τὸ
γλυκὺ[11] καὶ τὸ πικρόν[12]; **12** μὴ[13] δύναται, ἀδελφοί μου,
συκῆ[14] ἐλαίας[15] ποιῆσαι[16] ἢ ἄμπελος[17] σῦκα[18]; οὔτε
ἁλυκὸν[19] γλυκὺ[20] ποιῆσαι ὕδωρ[21].

13 Τίς σοφὸς[22] καὶ ἐπιστήμων[1] ἐν ὑμῖν; δειξάτω[2] ἐκ τῆς

---

[1] MH: pf. act. prtc. acc. masc. pl. from γίνομαι = root + prtc. morpheme + acc. masc. pl. ending (γεγον + ότ + ας). TH: Subst. prtc., *the ones having been made*.

[2] εὐλογία, -ας, ἡ, *a blessing*. TH: Nom. subject of ἐξέρχεται.

[3] κατάρα, -ας, ἡ, *a curse*. TH: Nom. subject of ἐξέρχεται.

[4] χρή, *it is necessary, it ought*. TH:

[5] TH: nom. neut. pl. from dem. pron. οὗτος, *these things*.

[6] TH: pres. mid./pass. inf. from γίνομαι. Complementary inf. completing χρή, *ought not be*.

[7] μήτι, interrogative particle in questions expecting a negative answer.

[8] πηγή, -ῆς, ἡ, *a spring, fountain*.

[9] ὀπή, -ῆς, ἡ, *opening, hole*. TH: ἐκ τῆς αὐτῆς ὀπῆς, prep. phrase of source, *from*.

[10] βρύω, *I pour forth*.

[11] γλυκύς, -εια, -ύ, *sweet*.

[12] πικρός, -ά, -όν, *bitter*.

[13] TH: μή, used in questions expecting a negative answer.

[14] συκῆ, -ῆς, ἡ, *a fig tree*. TH: Nom. subject of δύναται.

[15] ἐλαία, -ας, ἡ, *an olive tree*. TH: Dir. obj. of ποιῆσαι.

[16] MH: aor. act. inf. from ποιέω = root + aor. act. inf. morpheme (ποιῆ + σαι). Vowel lengthens in contract verb (ε › η).

[17] ἄμπελος, -ου, ἡ, *vine*. TH: Nom. subject of an implied δύναται ποιῆσαι, *a vine able to produce?*

[18] συκῆ, -ῆς, ἡ, *a fig tree*. TH: Dir. obj. of an implied δύναται ποιῆσαι, *able to produce figs?*

[19] ἁλυκός, -ή, -όν, *salty*. TH: Nom. subject of another implied δύναται, this time with the inf. complement repeated.

[20] γλυκύς, -εια, -ύ, *sweet*.

[21] TH: ἁλυκὸν is a substantive functioning as the subject with the implied ὕδωρ, thus *neither can salt water produce fresh water*.

[22] σοφός, -ή, -όν, *skillful, wise*. TH: Pred. adj. σοφός in equative clause with nom.

καλῆς ἀναστροφῆς[3] τὰ ἔργα αὐτοῦ ἐν πραΰτητι[4] σοφίας.
14 εἰ δὲ ζῆλον[5] πικρὸν[6] ἔχετε καὶ ἐριθείαν[7] ἐν τῇ καρδίᾳ
ὑμῶν[8], μὴ κατακαυχᾶσθε[9] καὶ ψεύδεσθε[10] κατὰ τῆς
ἀληθείας. **15** οὐκ ἔστιν αὕτη[11] ἡ σοφία ἄνωθεν[12]
κατερχομένη[13], ἀλλὰ ἐπίγειος[14], ψυχική[15], δαιμονιώδης[16].
16 ὅπου γὰρ ζῆλος[17] καὶ ἐριθεία[1], ἐκεῖ ἀκαταστασία[2] καὶ

---

subj. τίς.

1 ἐπιστήμων, -ον, *expert, skilled, understanding.* TH: Pred. adj. ἐπιστήμων in equative clause with nom. subj. τίς.

2 δείκνυμι, *I show, point out, make known.* MH: aor. act. impv. 3rd sg. from δείκνυμι = root + tense formative + act. 3rd sg. ending (δεικ + σά + τω). Review Square of Stops, k + σ › ξ.

3 ἀναστροφή, -ῆς, ἡ, *conduct.* TH: ἐκ τῆς καλῆς ἀναστροφῆς, prep. phrase of means, *by (means of).*

4 πραΰτης, -ητος, ἡ, *gentleness, humility, courtesy.* TH: ἐν πραΰτητι σοφίας, prep. phrase of manner modifying δειξάτω, *in (a manner of) gentleness that comes from wisdom.* Or, prep. phrase modifying τὰ ἔργα αὐτοῦ, *deeds of gentleness that comes from wisdom.*

5 ζῆλος, -ου, ὁ, *zeal, jealousy.*

6 πικρός, -ά, -όν, *bitter.*

7 ἐριθεία, -ας, ἡ, *rivalry, ambition.*

8 TH: ἐν τῇ καρδίᾳ ὑμῶν, spatial prep. phrase, *in* or *within.* Ὑμῶν, gen. of poss., *your heart.*

9 κατακαυχάομαι, *I exult over, triumph over.* TH: pres. mid. impv. 2nd pl. from κατακαυχάομαι.

10 ψεύδομαι, *I lie.* TH: pres. mid. impv. 2nd pl. from ψεύδομαι.

11 TH: Nom. subject of ἔστιν.

12 ἄνωθεν, *from above, again.* TH: ἡ σοφία is pred. adj. of ἔστιν + ἄνωθεν (spatial adv.), *wisdom from above.*

13 κατέρχομαι, *I come down, go down.* MH: pres. mid. prtc. nom. fem. sg. from κατέρχομαι = pre. (κατά) + root + connecting vowel + mid./pass. prtc. morpheme + nom. fem. sg. ending (κατ + ερχ + ο + μέν + η). TH: Attrib. adj. prtc. modifying ἡ σοφία, *wisdom which comes down.*

14 ἐπίγειος, -ον, *of the earth, earthly.* TH: Pred. adj. of implied ἔστιν.

15 ψυχικός, -ή, -όν, *natural, wordly-minded.* TH: Pred. adj. of implied ἔστιν.

16 δαιμονιώδης, -ες, *demonic, devilish.* TH: Pred. adj. of implied ἔστιν.

17 ζῆλος, -ου, ὁ, *zeal, jealousy.* TH: Nom. subject of implied ἔστιν.

πᾶν φαῦλον[3] πρᾶγμα[4]. **17** ἡ δὲ ἄνωθεν[5] σοφία πρῶτον[6] μὲν
ἁγνή[7] ἐστιν, ἔπειτα[8] εἰρηνική[9], ἐπιεικής[10], εὐπειθής[11],
μεστὴ[12] ἐλέους[13] καὶ καρπῶν ἀγαθῶν, ⸀ἀδιάκριτος[14],
ἀνυπόκριτος[15]· **18** καρπὸς ⸀δὲ δικαιοσύνης[16] ἐν εἰρήνῃ
σπείρεται τοῖς ποιοῦσιν[17] εἰρήνην.

---

[1] ἐριθεία, -ας, ἡ, *rivalry, ambition.* TH: Nom. subject of implied ἔστιν.

[2] ἀκαταστασία, -ας, ἡ, *a disturbance, disorder, tumult.* TH: Nom. subject of implied ἔστιν.

[3] φαῦλος, -η, -ον, *worthless, bad.*

[4] πρᾶγμα, -τος, τό, *a deed, matter, thing.* TH: Nom. subject of implied ἔστιν.

[5] ἄνωθεν, *from above, again.*

[6] TH: πρῶτον can be used to begin a series ordered according to prominence or sequence.

[7] ἁγνός, -ή, -όν, *pure, holy, chaste, innocent.*

[8] ἔπειτα, *then.*

[9] εἰρηνικός, -ή, -όν, *peaceable, peaceful.*

[10] ἐπιεικής, -ές, *yielding, gentle, kind, courteous.*

[11] εὐπειθής, -ές, *compliant, obedient.*

[12] μεστός, -ή, -όν, *full.*

[13] ἔλεος, -ους, τό, *pity, mercy, compassion.* TH: ἐλέους καὶ καρπῶν ἀγαθῶν, gen. of content, *full of mercy and good fruits.*

[14] ἀδιάκριτος, -ον, *unwavering.*

[15] ἀνυπόκριτος, -ον, *sincere, without hypocrisy, genuine.*

[16] TH: καρπὸς δικαιοσύνης, subjective gen., *fruit which is produced by righteousness.*

[17] TH: pres. act. prtc. dat. masc. pl. from ποιέω. Subst. prtc. and dative of agency, *by those who do/make peace.*

SBLGNT Sigla Apparatus for James 3

⸂ **3:3 εἰ δὲ** WH Treg NA28] Ἴδε RP

⸃ **3:3 εἰ δὲ** WH Treg NA28] Ἴδε RP

⸀ • **εἰς** WH Treg NA28] πρὸς RP

⸂ **4 ἀνέμων σκληρῶν** WH Treg NA28] σκληρῶν ἀνέμων RP

⸃ **4 ἀνέμων σκληρῶν** WH Treg NA28] σκληρῶν ἀνέμων RP

⸂ • **ἡ … βούλεται** WH Treg NA28] ἂν ἡ … βούληται RP

⸃ • **ἡ … βούλεται** WH Treg NA28] ἂν ἡ … βούληται RP

⸂ **5 μεγάλα αὐχεῖ** WH Treg NA28] μεγαλαυχεῖ RP

⸃ **5 μεγάλα αὐχεῖ** WH Treg NA28] μεγαλαυχεῖ RP

⸀ • **ἡλίκον** WH Treg NA28] ὀλίγον RP

⸆ **6 ἀδικίας** WH Treg NA28] + οὕτως RP

⸂ **8 δαμάσαι δύναται ἀνθρώπων** WH Treg NA28] δύναται ἀνθρώπων δαμάσαι RP

⸃ **8 δαμάσαι δύναται ἀνθρώπων** WH Treg NA28] δύναται ἀνθρώπων δαμάσαι RP

⸀ • **ἀκατάστατον** WH Treg NA28] ἀκατάσχετον RP

⸀ **9 κύριον** WH Treg NA28] θεὸν RP

⸂ **12 οὔτε ἁλυκὸν** WH Treg NA28] Οὕτως οὐδεμια πηγὴ ἁλυκὸν καὶ RP

⸃ **12 οὔτε ἁλυκὸν** WH Treg NA28] Οὕτως οὐδεμια πηγὴ ἁλυκὸν καὶ RP

⸆ **17 ἀδιάκριτος** WH Treg NA28] + καὶ RP

⸆ **18 δὲ** WH Treg NA28] + τῆς RP

JAMES 4

NEW VOCABULARY BY FREQUENCY
[Chapter, Book, SBLGNT Occurrences]

ἁμαρτωλός, -όν, *sinful, (subst.) sinner* [1, 2, 47]
ἐγγίζω, *I draw near, approach* [2, 3, 42]
ὀλίγος, -η, -ον, *little, small, few* [1, 1, 41]
σήμερον, *today* [1, 1, 41]
κλαίω, *I weep (for), lament* [1, 2, 40]
ὑποτάσσω, *I arrange under, put in subjection* [1, 1, 38]
βούλομαι, *I wish; I intend* [1, 3, 37]
διάβολος, -ου, *slanderous, accuser,* (subst.) *the Devil* [1, 1, 37]
μέλος, -ους, τό, *limb, member, (body) part* [1, 3, 34]
ποῖος, -α, -ον, *of what kind? which?* [1, 1, 33]
ἐχθρός, -ή, -όν, *hated, hostile,* (subst.) *an enemy* [1, 1, 32]
καθαρίζω, *I make clean, cleanse* [1, 1, 31]
φαίνω, *I bring to light, shine; I appear* [1, 1, 31]
πόθεν, *whence? from where?* [2, 2, 29]
φεύγω, *I flee (from); I escape* [1, 1, 29]
φίλος, -ου, ὁ, *loved, dear,* (subst.) *friend* [1, 2, 29]
διότι, *because, wherefore* [1, 1, 23]
ἀντί, (gen.) *over against, in place of, for* [1, 1, 22]
καθίστημι, *I set down; I set in order, appoint* [1, 2, 21]
ὑψόω, *I lift up, exalt* [1, 1, 20]
κριτής, -ου, ὁ, *a judge* [2, 4, 19]
πόλεμος, -ου, ὁ, *a war* [1, 1, 18]
κερδαίνω, *I gain* [1, 1, 17]
πλησίον, *near,* (subst.) *a neighbor* [1, 2, 17]
ἔπειτα, *then* [1, 2, 16]
ἐπιθυμέω, *I desire* [1, 1, 16]
κακῶς, *badly* [1, 1, 16]
ἀνθίστημι, *I resist, oppose* [1, 1, 14]
αὔριον, *tomorrow* [2, 2, 14]
ἐνιαυτός, -οῦ, ὁ, *a year* [1, 2, 14]
ἐπίσταμαι, *I understand, know* [1, 1, 14]
ταπεινόω, *to humble* [1, 1, 14]

φονεύω, *I kill, murder* [1, 4, 12]
ζηλόω, *to be zealous* [1, 1, 11]
καύχησις, -εως, ἡ, *boasting* [1, 1, 11]
ἐντεῦθεν, *hence, on each side, thereupon* [1, 1, 10]
ὅδε, ἥδε, τόδε, *this (here)* [1, 1, 10]
πενθέω, *I mourn* [1, 1, 10]
ἐπιποθέω, *to long for* [1, 1, 9]
φθόνος, -ου, ὁ, *envy* [1, 1, 9]
ταπεινός, -ή, -όν, *humble, downcast* [1, 2, 8]
ἁγνίζω, *I purify, cleanse from defilement* [1, 1, 7]
μοιχαλίς, -ίδος, ἡ, *an adulteress* [1, 1, 7]
πολεμέω, *I wage war* [1, 1, 7]
στρατεύομαι, *I make war, hence to serve as a soldier* [1, 1, 7]
ἔχθρα, -ας, ἡ, *enmity, hostility* [1, 1, 6]
ποιητής, -οῦ, ὁ, *a maker, a doer* [1, 4, 6]
ἀντιτάσσομαι, *I range in battle against, I oppose, resist* [1, 2, 5]
ἀφανίζω, *I destroy* [1, 1, 5]
δαπανάω, *I spend, spend freely* [1, 1, 5]
ἐπιτυγχάνω, *I obtain* [1, 1, 5]
ἡδονή, -ῆς, ἡ, *pleasure* [2, 2, 5]
καταλαλέω, *I speak evil of, slander* [3, 3, 5]
πένθος, -ους, τό, *mourning* [1, 1, 5]
ὑπερήφανος, -ον, *arrogant, haughty, proud* [1, 1, 5]
μάχη, -ης, ἡ, *a fight, conflict* [1, 1, 4]
μάχομαι, *I fight, quarrel* [1, 1, 4]
ἀλαζονεία, -ας, ἡ, *pretension, arrogance* [1, 1, 2]
ἀτμίς, -ίδος, ἡ, *vapor* [1, 1, 2]
δίψυχος, -ον, *double-minded, hesitating* [1, 2, 2]
ἐμπορεύομαι, *I engage in business* [1, 1, 2]
γέλως, -ωτος, ὁ, *laughter* [1, 1, 1]
κατήφεια, -ας, ἡ, *gloominess, dejection* [1, 1, 1]
κατοικίζω, *I cause to dwell* [1, 1, 1]
κενῶς, *to no purpose, in vain* [1, 1, 1]
μετατρέπω, *I turn around* [1, 1, 1]
νομοθέτης, -ου, ὁ, *a lawgiver* [1, 1, 1]
ταλαιπωρέω, *I endure hardship, to be miserable* [1, 1, 1]
φιλία, -ας, ἡ, *friendship, love* [1, 1, 1]

4.1 Πόθεν[1] πόλεμοι[2] καὶ ʹπόθεν[3] μάχαι[4] ἐν ὑμῖν; οὐκ
ἐντεῦθεν[5], ἐκ τῶν ἡδονῶν[6] ὑμῶν τῶν στρατευομένων[7] ἐν
τοῖς μέλεσιν[8] ὑμῶν; **2** ἐπιθυμεῖτε[9], καὶ οὐκ ἔχετε·
φονεύετε[10] καὶ ζηλοῦτε[11], καὶ οὐ δύνασθε ἐπιτυχεῖν[12]·
μάχεσθε[13] καὶ πολεμεῖτε[14]. οὐκ ἔχετε διὰ τὸ μὴ αἰτεῖσθαι
ὑμᾶς[15]· **3** αἰτεῖτε καὶ οὐ λαμβάνετε, διότι[16] κακῶς[17]
αἰτεῖσθε, ἵνα ἐν ταῖς ἡδοναῖς[18] ὑμῶν δαπανήσητε[19].

---

[1] πόθεν, *whence? from where?*
[2] πόλεμος, -ου, ὁ, *a war.*
[3] πόθεν, *whence? from where?*
[4] μάχη, -ης, ἡ, *a fight, conflict.*
[5] ἐντεῦθεν, *hence, on each side, thereupon,* ***from this***.
[6] ἡδονή, -ῆς, ἡ, *pleasure.* TH: ἐκ τῶν ἡδονῶν, prep. prhase of source in app. to ἐντεῦθεν.
[7] στρατεύομαι, *I make war, hence to serve as a soldier.* TH: pres. mid. prtc. gen. fem. pl. Attrib. adj. prtc. modifying τῶν ἡδονῶν ὑμῶν, *which make war.*
[8] μέλος, -ους, τό, *limb, member, (body) part.* TH: prep. phrase of location, *in/among your members.*
[9] ἐπιθυμέω, *I desire.*
[10] φονεύω, *I kill, murder.*
[11] ζηλόω, *to be zealous.*
[12] ἐπιτυγχάνω, *I obtain.* MH: aor. act. inf. = pre. (ἐπί) + root + aor. act. inf. morpheme (ἐπι + τυχ + εῖν). TH: Complementary inf. completing δύνασθε, *not able to obtain.*
[13] μάχομαι, *I fight, quarrel.*
[14] πολεμέω, *I wage war.*
[15] TH: διὰ τὸ μὴ αἰτεῖσθαι ὑμᾶς. διά + articular inf. = causal, *because.* Inf. often takes acc. subject, *you do not ask.*
[16] διότι, *because, wherefore.*
[17] κακῶς, *badly.*
[18] ἡδονή, -ῆς, ἡ, *pleasure.* TH: ἐν ταῖς ἡδοναῖς, prep. phrase of respect, *with respect to/on your pleasures.*
[19] δαπανάω, *I spend, spend freely.* MH: aor. act. subj. 2nd pl. = root + tense formative + length. connecting vowel + act. 2nd pl. ending (δαπανή + σ + η + τε). TH: ἵνα + subjunctive = purpose, *in order that.*

4 ⸀μοιχαλίδες[1], οὐκ[2] οἴδατε ὅτι[3] ἡ φιλία[4] τοῦ κόσμου[5]
ἔχθρα[6] τοῦ θεοῦ[7] ἐστιν; ὃς ⸀ἐὰν οὖν βουληθῇ[8] φίλος[9] εἶναι[10]
τοῦ κόσμου, ἐχθρὸς[11] τοῦ θεοῦ καθίσταται[12]. **5** ἢ δοκεῖτε
ὅτι[13] κενῶς[14] ἡ γραφὴ λέγει· Πρὸς φθόνον[15] ἐπιποθεῖ[16] τὸ
πνεῦμα ὃ ⸀κατῴκισεν[17] ἐν ἡμῖν; **6** μείζονα δὲ δίδωσιν[18]
χάριν· διὸ λέγει· Ὁ θεὸς ὑπερηφάνοις[19] ἀντιτάσσεται[20]
ταπεινοῖς[21] δὲ δίδωσιν χάριν. **7** ὑποτάγητε[22] οὖν τῷ θεῷ·

---

[1] μοιχαλίς, -ίδος, ἡ, *an adulteress.*
[2] TH: Introducing question expecting a positive answer.
[3] TH: ὅτι introducing the obj. clause of οἴδατε.
[4] φιλία, -ας, ἡ, *friendship, love.*
[5] TH: Obj. gen., *friendship with the world, love for the world.*
[6] ἔχθρα, -ας, ἡ, *enmity, hostility.*
[7] TH: Obj. gen., *hostility with God.*
[8] βούλομαι, *I wish, I intend.* MH: aor. pass. subj. 3rd sg. = root + length. connecting vowel + tense formative + pass. 3rd sg. ending (βουλ + η + θ + ῇ).
[9] φίλος, -ου, ὁ, *loved, dear*, (subst.) ***friend.***
[10] TH: pres. act. inf. from εἰμί. Complementary inf. completing βουληθῇ, *wishes to be.*
[11] ἐχθρός, -ή, -όν, *hated, hostile,* (subst.) *an enemy.*
[12] καθίστημι, *I set down; I set in order, appoint.* TH: pres. pass. indic. 3rd sg., *he is made an enemy.*
[13] TH: ὅτι introducing the obj. clause of δοκεῖτε.
[14] κενῶς, *to no purpose, in vain.*
[15] φθόνος, -ου, ὁ, *envy.* TH: πρὸς φθόνον, used as adverbial expression, *enviously.*
[16] ἐπιποθέω, *to long for.*
[17] κατοικίζω, *I cause to dwell.*
[18] MH: pres. act. indic. 3rd sg. from δίδωμι = root + connecting vowel + act. 3rd sg. ending (δίδ + ω + σιν).
[19] ὑπερήφανος, -ον, *arrogant, haughty, proud.* TH: Dat. complement of ἀντιτάσσεται.
[20] ἀντιτάσσομαι, *I range in battle against, I oppose, resist.*
[21] ταπεινός, -ή, -όν, *humble, downcast.* TH: Dat. indir. obj. of δίδωσιν.
[22] ὑποτάσσω, *I arrange under, put in subjection.* MH: aor. pass. impv. 2nd pl. from ὑποτάσσω = pref. (ὑπό) + root + tense formative + pass. 2nd pl. ending (ὑπο + τάγ + η + τε).

ἀντίστητε[1] δὲ τῷ διαβόλῳ[2], καὶ φεύξεται[3] ἀφ' ὑμῶν·
8 ἐγγίσατε[4] τῷ θεῷ, καὶ ⸀ἐγγιεῖ[5] ὑμῖν. καθαρίσατε[6]
χεῖρας, ἁμαρτωλοί[7], καὶ ἁγνίσατε[8] καρδίας, δίψυχοι[9].
9 ταλαιπωρήσατε[10] καὶ πενθήσατε[11] καὶ κλαύσατε[12]·
ὁ γέλως[13] ὑμῶν εἰς πένθος[14] ⸀μετατραπήτω[15] καὶ ἡ χαρὰ εἰς
κατήφειαν[16]· **10** ταπεινώθητε[17] ἐνώπιον ⸀κυρίου[18], καὶ
ὑψώσει[19] ὑμᾶς.

---

[1] ἀνθίστημι, *I resist, oppose.* MH: aor. act. impv. 2nd pl.
[2] διάβολος, -ου, *slanderous, accuser,* (subst.) *the Devil.*
[3] φεύγω, *I flee (from); I escape.* MH: fut. act. indic. 3rd sg. from φεύγω = root + tense formative + connecting vowel + act. 3rd sg. ending (φεύγ + σ + ε + ται). Review Square of Stops, γ + σ › ξ.
[4] ἐγγίζω, *I draw near, approach.* MH: aor. act. impv. 2nd pl.
[5] ἐγγίζω, *I draw near, approach.* MH: fut. act. indic. 3rd sg.
[6] καθαρίζω, *I make clean, cleanse.*
[7] ἁμαρτωλός, -όν, *sinful, (subst.) sinner.* TH: Voc., *sinners!*
[8] ἁγνίζω, *I purify, cleanse from defilement.*
[9] δίψυχος, -ον, *double-minded, hesitating.*
[10] ταλαιπωρέω, *I endure hardship, to be miserable.*
[11] πενθέω, *I mourn.*
[12] κλαίω, *I weep (for), lament.*
[13] γέλως, -ωτος, ὁ, *laughter.*
[14] πένθος, -ους, τό, *mourning.*
[15] μετατρέπω, *I turn around.* MH: aor. pass. impv. 3rd sg. from μετατρέπω = pref. (μετά) + root + connecting vowel + pass. 3rd sg. ending (μετα + τραπ + ή + τω). TH: ὁ γέλως functions as nom. subject, *let your laughter turn.*
[16] κατήφεια, -ας, ἡ, *gloominess, dejection.* TH: ἡ χαρὰ εἰς κατήφειαν mirrors previous clause with an implied μετατραπήτω, *let your joy turn.*
[17] ταπεινόω, *to humble.* MH: aor. pass. impv. 2nd pl. from ταπεινόω = root + length. connecting vowel (ο › ω) + tense formative + pass. 2nd pl. ending (ταπειν + ώ + θη + τε).
[18] NA[28] reads τοῦ κυρίου.
[19] ὑψόω, *I lift up, exalt.* MH: fut. act. indic. 3rd sg. from ὑψόω = root + length. contract vowel + tense formative + act. 3rd sg. ending (ὑψ + ώ + σ + ει). The vowel in a contract verb is length. before the tense formative (ο › ω).

11 Μὴ καταλαλεῖτε[1] ἀλλήλων, ἀδελφοί· ὁ καταλαλῶν[2]
ἀδελφοῦ[3] ⸀ἢ κρίνων[4] τὸν ἀδελφὸν αὐτοῦ καταλαλεῖ[5] νόμου[6]
καὶ κρίνει νόμον· εἰ δὲ νόμον κρίνεις, οὐκ εἶ[7] ποιητὴς[8]
νόμου ἀλλὰ κριτής[9]. **12** εἷς[10] ⸀ἐστιν[11] νομοθέτης[12] ⸂καὶ
κριτής[13]⸃, ὁ δυνάμενος[14] σῶσαι καὶ ἀπολέσαι[15]· σὺ δὲ τίς
εἶ[16], ⸂ὁ κρίνων[17]⸃ τὸν ⸀πλησίον[18];

---

[1] καταλαλέω, *I speak evil of, slander.*

[2] καταλαλέω, *I speak evil of, slander.* TH: pres. act. prtc. nom. masc. sg. from καταλαλέω. Subst. prtc. functioning as the subject of καταλαλεῖ, *the one who slanders.*

[3] TH: Obj. gen., *the one who slanders a brother.*

[4] TH: pres. act. prtc. nom. masc. sg. from κρίνω. Subst. prtc. functioning as the subject of καταλαλεῖ, *the one who judges.*

[5] καταλαλέω, *I speak evil of, slander.*

[6] TH: Obj. gen. functioning as object of καταλαλεῖ, *the one who slanders and judges…slanders the law.*

[7] TH: εἶ (the verb) may be easily confused with εἰ (conj. introducing conditional clause, *if*). Pres. act. indic. 2nd sg. from εἰμί, *you are.*

[8] ποιητής, -οῦ, ὁ, *a maker, a doer.*

[9] κριτής, -ου, ὁ, *a judge.*

[10] TH: Pred. nom. of ἐστιν, *there is one.*

[11] NA adds ὁ.

[12] νομοθέτης, -ου, ὁ, *a lawgiver.*

[13] κριτής, -ου, ὁ, *a judge.*

[14] TH: pres. mid. prtc. nom. masc. sg. from δύναμαι. Subst. prtc. functioning in app. to νομοθέτης καὶ κριτής, *the one who is able.*

[15] TH: σῶσαι καὶ ἀπολέσαι, aor. act. inf. from σῴζω and ἀπόλλυμι, respectively. Complementary inf. completing ὁ δυνάμενος, *the who is able to save and destroy.*

[16] TH: εἶ (the verb) may be easily confused with εἰ (conj. introducing conditional clause, *if*). Pres. act. indic. 2nd sg. from εἰμί, *you are.*

[17] TH: pres. act. prtc. nom. masc. sg. from κρίνω. Subst. prtc. functioning in app. to σὺ, *one who judges.*

[18] πλησίον, *near, (subst.)* ***a neighbor.***

13 Ἄγε νῦν[1] οἱ λέγοντες[2]· Σήμερον[3] ⸀ἢ αὔριον[4]
⸀πορευσόμεθα εἰς τήνδε[5] τὴν πόλιν καὶ ⸀ποιήσομεν ἐκεῖ
⸀ἐνιαυτὸν[6] καὶ ⸀ἐμπορευσόμεθα[7] καὶ ⸀κερδήσομεν[8]·
14 οἵτινες οὐκ ἐπίστασθε[9] ⸀τὸ τῆς αὔριον[10] ⸀ποία[11] ἡ ζωὴ
ὑμῶν· ἀτμὶς[12] γάρ ⸀ἐστε ⸀ἡ πρὸς ὀλίγον[13] φαινομένη[14],
⸀ἔπειτα[15] καὶ ἀφανιζομένη[16]· **15** ἀντὶ[17] τοῦ λέγειν ὑμᾶς·
Ἐὰν ὁ κύριος ⸀θελήσῃ[18], καὶ ⸀ζήσομεν καὶ ⸀ποιήσομεν
τοῦτο ἢ ἐκεῖνο. **16** νῦν δὲ καυχᾶσθε[19] ἐν ταῖς ἀλαζονείαις[1]

---

[1] TH: pres. act. impv. 2nd sg. from ἄγω + adverb νῦν = interjection, *come now!*
[2] TH: pres. act. prtc. nom. masc. pl. from λέγω. Subst. prtc., *the ones who say.*
[3] σήμερον, *today.*
[4] αὔριον, *tomorrow.*
[5] ὅδε, ἥδε, τόδε, *this (here),* ***such and such.***
[6] ἐνιαυτός, -οῦ, ὁ, *a year.* TH: acc. masc. sg. from ἐνιαυτός. Acc. of time indicating the extent of time, *for a year.*
[7] ἐμπορεύομαι, *I engage in business.*
[8] κερδαίνω, *I gain,* ***make a profit.***
[9] ἐπίσταμαι, *I understand, know.* MH: pres. mid. indic. 2nd pl. = root + mid. 2nd pl. ending (ἐπίστα + σθε).
[10] αὔριον, *tomorrow.* TH: τὸ τῆς αὔριον, *that which is of tomorrow.*
[11] ποῖος, -α, -ον, *of what kind? which?* TH: ποία ἡ ζωὴ ὑμῶν, clause standing in app. to τὸ τῆς αὔριον, *of what kind of life you live.*
[12] ἀτμίς, -ίδος, ἡ, *vapor.* TH: Pred. nom. of ἐστε, *you are a vapor.*
[13] ὀλίγος, -η, -ον, *little, small, few.*
[14] φαίνω, *I bring to light, shine; I appear.* TH: pres. pass. prtc. nom. fem. sg. Attrib. adj. prtc. modifying ἀτμίς, *which appears.*
[15] ἔπειτα, *then.*
[16] ἀφανίζω, *I destroy,* (pass. with act. sense) ***disappear.*** TH: pres. pass. prtc. nom. fem. sg. Attrib. adj. prtc. modifying ἀτμίς, ***which disappears.***
[17] ἀντί, (gen.) *over against, in place of, for.* TH: ἀντὶ τοῦ λέγειν ὑμᾶς, λέγειν is pres. act. inf. from λέγω. Acc. ὑμᾶς functions as subject of inf., *instead of you saying.*
[18] MH: aor. act. subj. 3rd sg. from θέλω = root + tense formative + act. 3rd sg. ending (θελή + σ + η).
[19] καυχάομαι, *I boast, am proud of.*

ὑμῶν· πᾶσα καύχησις[2] τοιαύτη πονηρά[3] ἐστιν. 17 εἰδότι[4]
οὖν καλὸν ποιεῖν καὶ μὴ ποιοῦντι[5], ἁμαρτία αὐτῷ[6] ἐστιν

SBLGNT SIGLA APPARATUS FOR JAMES 4

⸀ **4:1 πόθεν** WH Treg NA28] – RP
⸀ **4 μοιχαλίδες** WH Treg NA28] Μοιχοὶ καὶ μοιχαλίδες RP
⸀ • **ἐὰν** WH NA28] ἂν Treg RP
⸀ **5 κατῴκισεν** WH Treg NA28] κατῴκησεν RP
⸀ **8 ἐγγιεῖ** Treg NA28 RP] ἐγγίσει WH
⸀ **9 μετατραπήτω** WH NA28] μεταστραφήτω Treg RP
⸀ **10 κυρίου** WH Treg NA27] τοῦ κυρίου NA28 RP
⸀ **11 ἢ** WH Treg NA28] καὶ RP
⸀ **12 ἐστιν** WH] + ὁ Treg NA28 RP
⸂ • **καὶ κριτής** WH Treg NA28] – RP
⸃ • **καὶ κριτής** WH Treg NA28] – RP
⸂ • **ὁ κρίνων** WH Treg NA28] ὃς κρίνεις RP
⸃ • **ὁ κρίνων** WH Treg NA28] ὃς κρίνεις RP
⸀ • **πλησίον** WH Treg NA28] ἕτερον RP
⸀ **13 ἢ** WH Treg NA28] καὶ RP
⸀ • **πορευσόμεθα** WH Treg NA28] πορευσώμεθα RP
⸀ • **ποιήσομεν** WH NA28] ποιήσωμεν Treg RP
⸀ • **ἐνιαυτὸν** WH Treg NA28] + ἕνα RP
⸀ • **ἐμπορευσόμεθα** WH Treg NA28] ἐμπορευσώμεθα RP
⸀ • **κερδήσομεν** WH Treg NA28] κερδήσωμεν RP
⸀ **14 τὸ** Treg NA28 RP] – WH
⸀ • **ποία** WH NA28] + γὰρ Treg RP
⸀ • **ἐστε** WH Treg NA28] ἔσται RP
⸀ • **ἡ** Treg NA28 RP] – WH
⸀ • **ἔπειτα** WH Treg NA28] + δὲ RP
⸀ **15 θελήσῃ** Treg NA28 RP] θέλῃ WH
⸀ • **ζήσομεν** WH Treg NA28] ζήσωμεν RP
⸀ • **ποιήσομεν** WH Treg NA28] ποιήσωμεν RP

---

[1] ἀλαζονεία, -ας, ἡ, *pretension, arrogance.*

[2] καύχησις, -εως, ἡ, *boasting.* TH: πᾶσα καύχησις τοιαύτη, nom. subject of ἐστιν, *all boasting such as this is.*

[3] TH: Pred. adj. of ἐστιν, *is evil.*

[4] MH: pf. act. prtc. dat. masc. sg. from οἶδα = root + pf. act. prtc. morpheme + dat. masc. sg. ending (εἰδ + ότ + ι). TH: Subst. prtc., *one who knows.*

[5] MH: pres. act. prtc. dat. masc. sg. from ποιέω = root + contraction + pres. act. prtc. morpheme + dat. masc. sg. ending (ποι + οῦ + ντ + ι). Contractions according to vowel combinations (εο › ου). TH: Subst. prtc., *one who does.*

[6] TH: Dat. of disadvantage, *guilty of sin.*

JAMES 5

NEW VOCABULARY BY FREQUENCY

[Chapter, Book, SBLGNT Occurrences]

ἁμαρτωλός, -όν, *sinful, (subst.) sinner* [1, 2, 47]
πρό, (gen.) *before, in front of* [2, 2, 47]
κρίσις, -εως, ἡ, *judging, trial, judgment* [1, 3, 47]
ἐγγίζω, *I draw near, approach* [1, 3, 42]
κλαίω, *I weep (for), lament* [1, 2, 40]
τέλος, -ους, τό, *end, result, purpose* [1, 1, 40]
θύρα, -ας, ἡ, *door, gate* [1, 1, 39]
πλανάω, *I lead astray* [1, 2, 39]
ἐπιστρέφω, *I turn (around)* [2, 2, 36]
οὖς, ὠτός, τό, *ear* [1, 1, 36]
προσευχή, -ῆς, ἡ, *prayer* [1, 1, 36]
ἀσθενέω, *I am weak, feeble, sick* [1, 1, 34]
μήτε, *and not, neither … nor* [3, 3, 34]
ὑπομονή, -ῆς, ἡ, *patient endurance, perseverance* [1, 3, 32]
πλῆθος, -ους, τό, *a great number, multitude* [1, 1, 31]
Ἠλίας, -ου, ὁ, *Elijah* [1, 1, 29]
μισθός, -οῦ, ὁ, *wages, reward* [1, 1, 29]
προσκαλέω, *I summon,* (mid.) *call to oneself* [1, 1, 29]
ἰσχύω, *I am strong, able* [1, 1, 28]
πλούσιος, -α, -ον, *rich, wealthy* [1, 5, 28]
χώρα, -ας, ἡ, *country, region, field* [1, 1, 28]
ἰάομαι, *I heal, cure* [1, 1, 26]
ὀμνύω, *I vow, take an oath, swear* [1, 1, 26]
παρουσία, -ας, ἡ, *presence, arrival, coming* [2, 2, 24]
πλοῦτος, -ου, ὁ, *wealth, riches* [1, 1, 22]
ἐνεργέω, *I work, energize, operate* [1, 1, 21]
θερίζω, *I reap, harvest* [1, 1, 21]
μαρτύριον, -ου, τό, *testimony, proof* [1, 1, 20]
γεωργός, -οῦ, ὁ, *a farmer* [1, 1, 19]
κριτής, -ου, ὁ, *a judge* [1, 4, 19]
δέησις, -εως, ἡ, *an entreaty, prayer* [1, 1, 18]
μήν, μηνός, ὁ, *a month* [1, 1, 18]

ὑπομένω, *I tarry, endure* [1, 2, 17]
ἐργάτης, -ου, ὁ, *a workman, laborer* [1, 1, 16]
κἄν, *and if* [1, 1, 16]
ἐνιαυτός, -οῦ, ὁ, *a year* [1, 2, 14]
μακροθυμία, -ας, ἡ, *long-suffering, patience, forbearance* [1, 1, 14]
ἕξ, *six* [1, 1, 13]
στηρίζω, *I establish* [1, 1, 13]
τίμιος, -α, -ον, *precious, honorable* [1, 1, 13]
φονεύω, *I kill, murder* [1, 4, 12]
ἔλαιον, -ου, τό, *olive oil* [1, 1, 11]
ἐξομολογέω, *I confess, profess* [1, 1, 10]
μακροθυμέω, *to be patient* [3, 3, 10]
ὅρκος, -ου, ὁ, *an oath* [1, 1, 10]
πλάνη, -ης, ἡ, *a wandering, error* [1, 1, 10]
χρυσός, -οῦ, ὁ, *gold* [1, 1, 10]
ἀλείφω, *I anoint* [1, 1, 9]
ἐπέρχομαι, *I come to or upon* [1, 1, 9]
τρέφω, *I make to grow, I nourish, feed* [1, 1, 9]
θησαυρίζω, *I lay up, store up, treasure* [1, 1, 8]
καλύπτω, *I cover* [1, 1, 8]
βρέχω, *to send rain, to rain, to wet* [2, 2, 7]
εὔχομαι, *I pray* [1, 1, 7]
ἀποστερέω, *I defraud, deprive of* [1, 1, 6]
ἐκδέχομαι, *I await, expect* [1, 1, 6]
στενάζω, *I groan (within oneself), sigh deeply* [1, 1, 6]
ὑπόδειγμα, -τος, τό, *a copy, example* [1, 1, 6]
ἀντιτάσσομαι, *I range in battle against, I oppose, resist* [1, 2, 5]
ἄργυρος, -ου, ὁ, *silver* [1, 1, 5]
καταδικάζω, *I pass sentence upon, condemn* [1, 1, 5]
ὑετός, -ου, ὁ, *rain* [1, 1, 5]
ψάλλω, *I sing, sing praise* [1, 1, 5]
βλαστάνω, *to sprout, produce* [1, 1, 4]
εὐθυμέω, *I am cheerful* [1, 1, 3]
εὐχή, -ῆς, ἡ, *a prayer, vow* [1, 1, 3]
ἰός, -οῦ, ὁ, *rust, poison* [1, 2, 3]
οἰκτίρμων, -ον, *merciful* [1, 1, 3]
σφαγή, -ῆς, ἡ, *slaughter* [1, 1, 3]

κάμνω, *I am weary, ill* [1, 1, 2]
μακαρίζω, *to consider blessed, happy* [1, 1, 2]
ὁμοιοπαθής, -ές, *with the same nature* [1, 1, 2]
Σαβαώθ, *Sabaoth, Lord of the Armies, Lord of Hosts* [1, 1, 2]
σπαταλάω, *I live a life of self-indulgence or wanton luxury* [1, 1, 2]
ταλαιπωρία, -ας, ἡ, *distress, misery* [1, 1, 2]
ἀμάω, *I mow* [1, 1, 1]
βοή, -ῆς, ἡ, *an outcry, shout* [1, 1, 1]
'Ιώβ, ὁ, *Job* [1, 1, 1]
κακοπάθεια, -ας, ἡ, *suffering, affliction* [1, 1, 1]
κατιόομαι, *I become rusty, corroded* [1, 1, 1]
ὀλολύζω, *I cry out, wail* [1, 1, 1]
ὄψιμος, -ου, ὁ, *late rain, spring rain* [1, 1, 1]
πολύσπλαγχνος, -ον, *sympathetic, compassionate, merciful* [1, 1, 1]
πρόϊμος, -ου, ὁ, *early rain, early crops* [1, 1, 1]
σήπω, *I decay, rot* [1, 1, 1]
σητόβρωτος, -ον, *moth-eaten* [1, 1, 1]
τρυφάω, *I live for pleasure, revel, carouse* [1, 1, 1]

GRAMMATICAL OVERVIEW FOR JAMES 5

In chapter 5, there is a high possibility for confusion between aor. 2nd pl. imperative and aor. 2nd pl. indicative verbs. James's frequent use of 2nd pl. imperatives (often aor.) may pose a challenge for beginning readers. In general, it may be helpful to review what distinguishes imperatives from indicative verbs. But, for the sake of this chapter's high repition of aor. 2nd pl. verbs specifically, the easiest distinguishing mark is the absence of an augment outside of the indicative mood. For example, in 5:5 the verb ἐτρυφήσατε is aor. act. indic. 2nd pl. Notice how the augment can help to confirm the verb is indicative. Likewise, in 5:8 the imperative verb στηρίξατε can be ruled out as an indicative because there is no augment in the aorist imperative (notice the tense formative).

5.1 Ἄγε νῦν[1] οἱ πλούσιοι[2], κλαύσατε[3] ὀλολύζοντες[4] ἐπὶ
ταῖς ταλαιπωρίαις[5] ὑμῶν ταῖς ἐπερχομέναις[6]. 2 ὁ πλοῦτος[7]
ὑμῶν σέσηπεν[8], καὶ τὰ ἱμάτια ὑμῶν σητόβρωτα[9] γέγονεν,
3 ὁ χρυσὸς[10] ὑμῶν καὶ ὁ ἄργυρος[11] κατίωται[12], καὶ ὁ ἰὸς[13]
αὐτῶν εἰς μαρτύριον[14] ὑμῖν[15] ἔσται καὶ φάγεται[16] τὰς
σάρκας ὑμῶν· ὡς πῦρ ἐθησαυρίσατε[17] ἐν ἐσχάταις
ἡμέραις[18]. 4 ἰδοὺ ὁ μισθὸς[19] τῶν ἐργατῶν[20] τῶν ἀμησάντων[21]

---

[1] TH: pres. act. impv. 2nd sg. from ἄγω + adverb νῦν = interjection, *come now!*

[2] πλούσιος, -α, -ον, *rich, wealthy*. TH: voc. masc. pl. Adj. used subst., *rich people*.

[3] κλαίω, *I weep (for), lament*.

[4] ὀλολύζω, *I cry out, wail*. TH: pres. act. prtc. nom. masc. pl. Adv. prtc. of manner modifying κλαύσατε, *weep by crying out*.

[5] ταλαιπωρία, -ας, ἡ, *distress, misery*. TH: ἐπὶ + dat. can indicate cause, *because of your miseries*.

[6] ἐπέρχομαι, *I come to or upon*. MH: pres. mid. prtc. dat. fem. pl. = pref. (ἐπί) + root + connecting vowel + mid. prtc. morpheme + dat. fem. pl. ending (ἐπ + ερχ + ο + μέν + αις). TH: Attrib. adj. prtc. modifying ταῖς ταλαιπωρίαις, *which are coming*.

[7] πλοῦτος, -ου, ὁ, *wealth, riches*.

[8] σήπω, *I decay, rot*.

[9] σητόβρωτος, -ον, *moth-eaten*. TH: Pred. adj. of γέγονεν.

[10] χρυσός, -οῦ, ὁ, *gold*.

[11] ἄργυρος, -ου, ὁ, *silver*.

[12] κατιόομαι, *I become rusty, corroded*.

[13] ἰός, -οῦ, ὁ, *rust, poison*.

[14] μαρτύριον, -ου, τό, *testimony, proof*. TH: εἰς μαρτύριον, *as evidence*.

[15] TH: Dat. of disadvantage, *evidence against you*.

[16] MH: fut. mid. indic. 3rd sg. from ἐσθίω = root + connecting vowel + mid. 3rd sg. ending (φάγ + ε + ται). The fut. and aor. root for ἐσθίω is φάγ-.

[17] θησαυρίζω, *I lay up, store up, treasure*.

[18] TH: ἐν + dat. (ἐσχάταις ἡμέραις) used temporally, *in the last days*.

[19] μισθός, -οῦ, ὁ, *wages, reward*. TH: Functions as the subject of κράζει, found at the end of the clause.

[20] ἐργάτης, -ου, ὁ, *a workman, laborer*. TH: Poss. gen., *the workers' wages*.

[21] ἀμάω, *I mow*. TH: aor. act. prtc. gen. masc. pl. Attrib. adj. prtc. modifying τῶν ἐργατῶν, *who mowed*.

τὰς χώρας[1] ὑμῶν ὁ ⸀ἀφυστερημένος[2] ἀφ᾽ ὑμῶν[3] κράζει, καὶ
αἱ βοαὶ[4] τῶν θερισάντων[5] εἰς τὰ ὦτα[6] Κυρίου Σαβαὼθ[7]
⸀εἰσεληλύθασιν[8]· **5** ἐτρυφήσατε[9] ἐπὶ τῆς γῆς καὶ
ἐσπαταλήσατε[10], ἐθρέψατε[11] τὰς καρδίας ⸀ὑμῶν ἐν ἡμέρᾳ
σφαγῆς[12]. **6** κατεδικάσατε[13], ἐφονεύσατε[14] τὸν δίκαιον[15].
οὐκ ἀντιτάσσεται[16] ὑμῖν;

7 Μακροθυμήσατε[17] οὖν, ἀδελφοί, ἕως τῆς παρουσίας[18]

---

[1] χώρα, -ας, ἡ, *country, region,* ***field***.
[2] ἀποστερέω, *I defraud, deprive of,* (pass.) ***stolen***. TH: pf. pass. prtc. nom. masc. sg. Attrib. adj. prtc. modifying ὁ μισθὸς, *which have been stolen*. NA has ἀπεστερημένος.
[3] TH: ἀφ᾽ ὑμῶν, *by you.*
[4] βοή, -ῆς, ἡ, *an outcry, shout.* TH: Nom. subject of εἰσεληλύθασιν, *the outcries...have come to.*
[5] θερίζω, *I reap, harvest.* TH: aor. act. prtc. gen. masc. pl. Subst. prtc., *the ones who harvested.*
[6] οὖς, ὠτός, τό, *ear.*
[7] Σαβαώθ, *Sabaoth, Lord of the Armies, Lord of Hosts.*
[8] MH: pf. act. indic. 3rd pl. from εἰσέρχομαι = pref. (εἰς) + root + act. 3rd pl. ending (εἰσ + εληλύθα + σιν).
[9] τρυφάω, *I live for pleasure, revel, carouse.* MH: aor. act. indic. 2nd pl. = aug. + root + length. contract vowel + tense formative + act. 2nd pl. ending (ἐ + τρυφ + ή + σα + τε). The vowel in a contract verb is length. before the tense formative (ε › η).
[10] σπαταλάω, *I live a life of self-indulgence or wanton luxury.*
[11] τρέφω, *I make to grow, I nourish, feed.*
[12] σφαγή, -ῆς, ἡ, *slaughter.*
[13] καταδικάζω, *I pass sentence upon, condemn.*
[14] φονεύω, *I kill, murder.*
[15] TH: acc. masc. sg. (dir. obj.) from δικαιος. Used subst., *the righteous one, the righteous man.*
[16] ἀντιτάσσομαι, *I range in battle against, I oppose, resist.* TH: Takes a dat. complement, *he does not resist you.*
[17] μακροθυμέω, *to be patient.* MH: aor. act. impv. 2nd pl.
[18] παρουσία, -ας, ἡ, *presence, arrival, coming.*

τοῦ κυρίου. ἰδοὺ ὁ γεωργὸς[1] ἐκδέχεται[2] τὸν τίμιον[3]
καρπὸν τῆς γῆς[4], μακροθυμῶν[5] ἐπ' ⸀αὐτῷ[6] ἕως ⸀λάβῃ
πρόϊμον[7] καὶ ὄψιμον[8]. **8** μακροθυμήσατε[9] καὶ ὑμεῖς,
στηρίξατε[10] τὰς καρδίας ὑμῶν[11], ὅτι[12] ἡ παρουσία[13] τοῦ
κυρίου ἤγγικεν[14]. **9** μὴ στενάζετε[15], ⸀ἀδελφοί, κατ'
ἀλλήλων⸌, ἵνα μὴ κριθῆτε[16]· ἰδοὺ ὁ κριτὴς[17] πρὸ[18] τῶν
θυρῶν[19] ἕστηκεν[20]. **10** ὑπόδειγμα[21] λάβετε, ⸀ἀδελφοί, τῆς

---

[1] γεωργός, -οῦ, ὁ, *a farmer.*
[2] ἐκδέχομαι, *I await, expect.*
[3] τίμιος, -α, -ον, *precious, honorable.*
[4] TH: Gen. of source, *fruit which comes from the earth.*
[5] μακροθυμέω, *to be patient.* TH: pres. act. prtc. nom. masc. sg. Prtc. of attendant circumstance, *as he is patient.*
[6] TH: ἐπί + dat. used to convey motive/reason, *for it* (where the antecendent αὐτῷ is καρπὸν, *the crop/fruit*).
[7] πρόϊμος, -ου, ὁ, *early rain, early crops.*
[8] ὄψιμος, -ου, ὁ, *late rain, spring rain.*
[9] μακροθυμέω, *to be patient.* MH: aor. act. impv. 2nd pl.
[10] στηρίζω, *I establish.* MH: aor. act. impv. 2nd pl.
[11] TH: Poss. gen., *your hearts.*
[12] TH: Causal usage of conj. ὅτι, *because.*
[13] παρουσία, -ας, ἡ, *presence, arrival, coming.*
[14] ἐγγίζω, *I draw near, approach.* MH: pf. act. indic. 3rd sg. = vocalic redupl. + root + tense formative + act. 3rd sg. ending (ἤ + γγι + κε + ν). In pf. tense verb beg. with a vowel, redupl. can take the form of a length. vowel (ε › η).
[15] στενάζω, *I groan (within oneself), sigh deeply,* ***complain***. TH: pres. act. impv. 2nd pl. Prohibitive impv., *do not complain.*
[16] TH: aor. pass. subj. 2nd pl. from κρίνω. ἵνα + subj. = purpose clause, *in order that you might not be judged.*
[17] κριτής, -ου, ὁ, *a judge.*
[18] πρό, (gen.) *before, in front of.*
[19] θύρα, -ας, ἡ, *door, gate.*
[20] MH: pf. act. indic. 3rd sg. from ἵστημι = vocalic redup. + root + tense formative + act. 3rd sg. ending (ἕ + στη + κε + ν). In pf. tense verb beg. with a vowel, redupl. can take the form of a length. vowel (ι › η).
[21] ὑπόδειγμα, -τος, τό, *a copy, example.* TH: First acc. (ὑπόδειγμα) in a double

κακοπαθίας[1] καὶ τῆς μακροθυμίας[2] τοὺς προφήτας,
οἳ ἐλάλησαν[3] ⸀ἐν τῷ ὀνόματι κυρίου. **11** ἰδοὺ μακαρίζομεν[4]
τοὺς ⸀ὑπομείναντας[5]· τὴν ὑπομονὴν[6] Ἰὼβ[7] ἠκούσατε, καὶ
τὸ τέλος[8] κυρίου ⸀εἴδετε[9], ὅτι[10] πολύσπλαγχνός[11] ἐστιν
⸂ὁ κύριος⸃ καὶ οἰκτίρμων[12].

12 Πρὸ[13] πάντων δέ, ἀδελφοί μου, μὴ ὀμνύετε[14], μήτε[15]
τὸν οὐρανὸν μήτε[16] τὴν γῆν μήτε[17] ἄλλον τινὰ ὅρκον[18]·

---

acc. constr. Second acc. is τοὺς προφήτας. Λάβετε, aor. act. impv. 2nd pl. from λαμβάνω, *take the prophets* (second acc.) *as an example* (first acc.)

[1] κακοπάθεια, -ας, ἡ, *suffering, affliction.*

[2] μακροθυμία, -ας, ἡ, *long-suffering, patience, forbearance.*

[3] TH: aor. act. indic. 3rd pl. from λαλέω. οἳ (rel. pron.) as nom. subject, *who spoke.*

[4] μακαρίζω, *to consider blessed, happy.*

[5] ὑπομένω, *I tarry, endure.* MH: aor. act. prtc. acc. masc. pl. = pref. (ὑπό) + root + tense formative + aor. act. prtc. morpheme + acc. masc. pl. ending (ὑπο + μείν + α + ντ + ας). Aor. tense formative (σα) drops the σ in a liquid verb (λ, μ, ν, or ρ). TH: Subst. prtc. as dir. obj. of μακαρίζομεν, *we consider blessed the ones who endured.*

[6] ὑπομονή, -ῆς, ἡ, *patient endurance, perseverance.*

[7] Ἰώβ, ὁ, *Job.*

[8] τέλος, -ους, τό, *end, result, purpose.*

[9] ὁράω, *I see.* MH: aor. act. indic. 2nd pl.

[10] TH: Conj. introducing epexegetical clause modifying τὸ τέλος κυρίου, *that* (introducing the content of the end/result of the Lord).

[11] πολύσπλαγχνος, -ον, *sympathetic, compassionate, merciful.*

[12] οἰκτίρμων, -ον, *merciful.*

[13] πρό, (gen.) *before, in front of.* TH: πρό + πάντων = idiomatic expression, *above all.*

[14] ὀμνύω, *I vow, take an oath, swear.* TH: pres. act. impv. 2nd pl. With acc. = swear an oath *by* something (οὐρανὸν…γῆν). Prohibitive impv., *do not swear an oath.*

[15] μήτε, *and not, neither … nor.*

[16] μήτε, *and not, neither … nor.*

[17] μήτε, *and not, neither … nor.*

[18] ὅρκος, -ου, ὁ, *an oath.*

ἤτω[1] δὲ ὑμῶν τὸ Ναὶ[2] ναὶ[3] καὶ τὸ Οὒ οὔ, ἵνα μὴ ⸀ὑπὸ
κρίσιν[4]⸁ πέσητε[5].

13 Κακοπαθεῖ[6] τις ἐν ὑμῖν; προσευχέσθω[7]· εὐθυμεῖ[8]
τις; ψαλλέτω[9]. **14** ἀσθενεῖ[10] τις ἐν ὑμῖν; προσκαλεσάσθω[11]
τοὺς πρεσβυτέρους τῆς ἐκκλησίας, καὶ προσευ-
ξάσθωσαν[12] ἐπ' αὐτὸν ἀλείψαντες[13] ⸀αὐτὸν ἐλαίῳ[14] ἐν τῷ
ὀνόματι τοῦ κυρίου· **15** καὶ ἡ εὐχὴ[15] τῆς πίστεως[16] σώσει[17]

---

[1] TH: pres. act. impv. 3rd sg. from εἰμί.

[2] ναί, *yes, certainly*. TH: Nom. subject of ἤτω. Mirrored in the verbless clause, τὸ Οὒ as nom. subject of implied ἤτω.

[3] ναί, *yes, certainly*. TH: Pred. nom. of ἤτω. Mirrored in the verbless clause, οὔ as pred. nom. of implied ἤτω.

[4] κρίσις, -εως, ἡ, *judging, trial, judgment.*

[5] TH: aor. act. subj. 2nd pl. from πίπτω. ἵνα + subj. = purpose, *in order that you might not fall.*

[6] κακοπαθέω, *I suffer hardship, misfortune.*

[7] TH: pres. mid. impv. 3rd sg. from προσεύχομαι.

[8] εὐθυμέω, *I am cheerful.*

[9] ψάλλω, *I sing, sing praise*. MH: pres. act. impv. 3rd sg.

[10] ἀσθενέω, *I am weak, feeble, sick.*

[11] προσκαλέω, *I summon,* (mid.) *call to oneself.* MH: aor. mid. impv. 3rd sg.

[12] MH: aor. mid. impv. 3rd pl. from προσεύχομαι = pref. (πρός) + root + tense formative + mid. 3rd pl. ending (προς + ευχ + σά + σθωσαν). Review Square of Stops, χ + σ › ξ.

[13] ἀλείφω, *I anoint*. TH: aor. act. prtc. nom. masc. pl. Prtc. of attendant circumstance, *as they anoint.*

[14] ἔλαιον, -ου, τό, *olive oil*. TH: Dat. of material, *with olive oil.*

[15] εὐχή, -ῆς, ἡ, *a prayer, vow.*

[16] TH: Attrib. gen., *faithful prayer*. Or, gen. of source, *prayer which comes from faith/faithfulness.* Or, more broadly, descriptive gen., *prayer which is characterized by faith/faithfulness.*

[17] TH: Although the initial gloss of σῴζω for beg. Greek students is *to save*, it can be used to mean “deliverance from illness”, *to heal.*

τὸν κάμνοντα[1], καὶ ἐγερεῖ[2] αὐτὸν ὁ κύριος· κἂν[3] ἁμαρτίας
ᾖ πεποιηκώς[4], ἀφεθήσεται[5] αὐτῷ. **16** ἐξομολογεῖσθε[6] ⸀οὖν
ἀλλήλοις ⸂τὰς ἁμαρτίας⸃ καὶ ⸀εὔχεσθε[7] ὑπὲρ ἀλλήλων, ὅπως
ἰαθῆτε[8]. πολὺ ἰσχύει[9] δέησις[10] δικαίου ἐνεργουμένη[11].
17 Ἠλίας[12] ἄνθρωπος ἦν ὁμοιοπαθὴς[13] ἡμῖν, καὶ
προσευχῇ[14] προσηύξατο τοῦ μὴ βρέξαι[15], καὶ οὐκ

---

[1] κάμνω, *I am weary, ill.* TH: pres. act. prtc. acc. masc. sg. Subst. prtc., *the one who is ill.*

[2] MH: fut. act. indic. 3rd sg. from ἐγείρω = root + absent tense formative + connecting vowel + act. 3rd sg. ending (ἐγερ + ε + ῖ). Liquid verbs (ending in λ, μ, ν, or ρ) drop the fut. tense formative (σ).

[3] κἄν, *and if.*

[4] TH: pf. act. prtc. nom. masc. sg. from ποιέω. ᾖ (pres. act. subj. 3rd sg. from εἰμί) + πεποιηκώς (pf. prtc.) = pf. periphr., *he has done/commited.*

[5] MH: fut. pass. indic. 3rd sg. from ἀφίημι = root + tense formative + connecting vowel + pass. 3rd sg. ending (ἀφε + θής + ε + ται). TH: Implied subject ἁμαρτίας, *it (the sins) will be forgiven to him.*

[6] ἐξομολογέω, *I confess, profess.* MH: pres. mid. impv. 2nd pl.

[7] εὔχομαι, *I pray.* MH: pres. mid. impv. 2nd pl.

[8] ἰάομαι, *I heal, cure.* TH: aor. pass. subj. 3rd sg. from ἰάομαι. ὅπως + subj. = purpose, *in order that you might be healed.*

[9] ἰσχύω, *I am strong, able.*

[10] δέησις, -εως, ἡ, *an entreaty, prayer.*

[11] ἐνεργέω, *I work, operate,* (mid.) ***in effect/operation***. TH: pres. mid. prtc. nom. fem. sg. Could be an adv. prtc. modifying ἰσχύει, *prayer… has much power as it is working* or adj. prtc. Modifying δέησις, *effective prayer.*

[12] Ἠλίας, -ου, ὁ, *Elijah.*

[13] ὁμοιοπαθής, -ές, *with the same nature.*

[14] προσευχή, -ῆς, ἡ, *prayer.* TH: προσευχῇ (dat. fem. sg. from προσευχή) + προσηύξατο (aor. mid. indic. 3rd sg. from προσεύχομαι) = *he prayed a prayer* (redundant), *he prayed.*

[15] βρέχω, *to send rain, to rain, to wet.* TH: Inf. indicating purpose, *he prayed (in order) to send rain.*

ἔβρεξεν[1] ἐπὶ τῆς γῆς ἐνιαυτοὺς[2] τρεῖς καὶ μῆνας[3] ἕξ[4]·
18 καὶ πάλιν προσηύξατο, καὶ ὁ οὐρανὸς ⸂ὑετὸν[5] ἔδωκεν[6]⸃
καὶ ἡ γῆ ἐβλάστησεν[7] τὸν καρπὸν αὐτῆς[8].

19 Ἀδελφοί ⸀μου, ἐάν τις ἐν ὑμῖν πλανηθῇ[9] ἀπὸ τῆς
ἀληθείας καὶ ἐπιστρέψῃ[10] τις αὐτόν, **20** ⸀γινωσκέτω[11] ὅτι[12]
ὁ ἐπιστρέψας[13] ἁμαρτωλὸν[14] ἐκ πλάνης[15] ὁδοῦ αὐτοῦ
σώσει[16] ψυχὴν ⸀αὐτοῦ ἐκ θανάτου καὶ καλύψει[17] πλῆθος[18]
ἁμαρτιῶν.

---

[1] βρέχω, *to send rain, to rain, to wet.*
[2] ἐνιαυτός, -οῦ, ὁ, *a year.* TH: Acc. of *extent of* time: *for three years and six months*
[3] μήν, μηνός, ὁ, *a month.*
[4] ἕξ, *six.*
[5] ὑετός, -ου, ὁ, *rain.*
[6] MH: aor. act. indic. 3rd sg. from δίδωμι = aug. + root + tense formative + act. 3rd sg. ending (ἐ + δω + κε + ν) -μι verbs often take κα as tense formative, as opposed to σα. Known as κ (kappa) aorist.
[7] βλαστάνω, *to sprout, produce.*
[8] TH: Poss. gen., its (the earth's) fruit.
[9] πλανάω, *I lead astray.* TH: aor. pass. subj. 3rd sg. from πλανάω.
[10] ἐπιστρέφω, *I turn (around).* TH: aor. act. subj. 3rd sg. from ἐπιστρέφω. Τις as nom. subject.
[11] TH: pres. act. impv. 3rd sg. from γινώσκω.
[12] TH: Conj. ὅτι introducing obj. of γινωσκέτω, *that.*
[13] ἐπιστρέφω, *I turn (around).* TH: aor. act. prtc. nom. masc. sg. from ἐπιστρέφω. Subst. prtc., *the one who turns.*
[14] ἁμαρτωλός, -όν, *sinful, (subst.) sinner.*
[15] πλάνη, -ης, ἡ, *a wandering, error.*
[16] TH: Nom. subject of σώσει is ὁ ἐπιστρέψας.
[17] καλύπτω, *I cover.* MH: fut. act. indic. 3rd sg. from καλύπτω = root + tense formative + act. 3rd sg. ending (καλύβ + σ + ει). Review Square of Stops, β + σ › ψ.
[18] πλῆθος, -ους, τό, *a great number, multitude.*

SBLGNT SIGLA APPARATUS FOR JAMES 5

⸀ **5:4 ἀφυστερημένος** WH Treg] ἀπεστερημένος NA28 RP
⸀ • **εἰσεληλύθασιν** NA28 RP] εἰσελήλυθαν WH Treg
⸀ **5 ὑμῶν** WH Treg NA28] + ὡς RP
⸀ **7 αὐτῷ** WH Treg NA28] αὐτόν RP
⸀ • **λάβῃ** WH Treg NA28] + ὑετὸν RP
⸂ **9 ἀδελφοί κατ' ἀλλήλων** WH Treg NA28] κατ' ἀλλήλων ἀδελφοί RP
⸃ **9 ἀδελφοί κατ' ἀλλήλων** WH Treg NA28] κατ' ἀλλήλων ἀδελφοί RP
⸀ **10 ἀδελφοί** WH Treg NA28] + μου RP
⸀ • **ἐν** WH Treg NA28] – RP
⸀ **11 ὑπομείναντας** WH Treg NA28] ὑπομένοντας RP
⸀ • **εἴδετε** WH Treg NA28] ἴδετε RP
⸂ • **ὁ κύριος** WH Treg NA28] – RP
⸃ • **ὁ κύριος** WH Treg NA28] – RP
⸂ **12 ὑπὸ κρίσιν** WH Treg NA28] εἰς ὑπὸκρίσιν RP
⸃ **12 ὑπὸ κρίσιν** WH Treg NA28] εἰς ὑπὸκρίσιν RP
⸀ **14 αὐτὸν** Treg NA28 RP] – WH
⸀ **16 οὖν** WH Treg NA28] – RP
⸂ • **τὰς ἁμαρτίας** WH Treg NA28] τὰ παραπτώματα RP
⸃ • **τὰς ἁμαρτίας** WH Treg NA28] τὰ παραπτώματα RP
⸀ • **εὔχεσθε** Treg NA28 RP] προσεύχεσθε WH
⸂ **18 ὑετὸν ἔδωκεν** WH NA28 RP] ἔδωκεν ὑετὸν Treg
⸃ **18 ὑετὸν ἔδωκεν** WH NA28 RP] ἔδωκεν ὑετὸν Treg
⸀ **19 μου** WH Treg NA28] – RP
⸀ **20 γινωσκέτω** Treg NA28 RP] γινώσκετε WH
⸀ • **αὐτοῦ** WH NA28] – Treg RP

Appendices

APPENDIX I
SBLGNT Apparatus

APPENDIX II
Vocabulary 50 times or more sorted by frequency

APPENDIX III
Vocabulary 50 times or more arranged alphabetically

APPENDIX IV
Paradigm Charts

JAMES 1

⸀ **1:5 μὴ** WH Treg NA28] οὐκ RP
⸀ **12 ἐπηγγείλατο** WH Treg NA28] + ὁ κύριος RP
⸀ **19 Ἴστε** WH Treg NA28] Ὥστε RP
⸀ • **δὲ** WH Treg NA28] – RP
⸂ **20 οὐκ ἐργάζεται** WH Treg NA27] οὐ κατεργάζεται NA28 RP
⸃ **20 οὐκ ἐργάζεται** WH Treg NA27] οὐ κατεργάζεται NA28 RP
⸂ **22 ἀκροαταὶ μόνον** WH Treg] μόνον ἀκροαταὶ NA28 RP
⸃ **22 ἀκροαταὶ μόνον** WH Treg] μόνον ἀκροαταὶ NA28 RP
⸀ **25 οὐκ** WH Treg NA28] οὗτος οὐκ RP
⸀ **26 εἶναι** WH Treg NA28] + ἐν ὑμῖν RP
⸀ • **αὐτοῦ** Treg NA28 RP] ἑαυτοῦ WH
⸀ • **αὐτοῦ** Treg NA28 RP] ἑαυτοῦ WH
⸀ **27 τῷ** WH Treg NA28] – RP

JAMES 2

⸀ **2:2 εἰς** WH Treg NA28] + τὴν RP
⸂ **3 ἐπιβλέψητε δὲ** WH NA28] καὶ ἐπιβλέψητε Treg RP
⸃ **3 ἐπιβλέψητε δὲ** WH NA28] καὶ ἐπιβλέψητε Treg RP
⸀ • **εἴπητε** WH Treg NA28] + αὐτῷ RP
⸂ • **ἢ κάθου ἐκεῖ** WH NA28] ἐκεῖ ἢ κάθου Treg NA27; ἐκεῖ ἢ κάθου ὧδε RP
⸃ • **ἢ κάθου ἐκεῖ** WH NA28] ἐκεῖ ἢ κάθου Treg NA27; ἐκεῖ ἢ κάθου ὧδε RP
⸀ **4 οὐ** WH Treg NA27] καὶ οὐ NA28 RP
⸂ **5 τῷ κόσμῳ** WH Treg NA28] τοῦ κόσμου RP
⸃ **5 τῷ κόσμῳ** WH Treg NA28] τοῦ κόσμου RP
⸂ **10 τηρήσῃ πταίσῃ** WH Treg NA28] τηρήσει πταίσει RP
⸃ **10 τηρήσῃ πταίσῃ** WH Treg NA28] τηρήσει πταίσει RP
⸀ **11 μοιχεύσῃς** WH Treg NA28] μοιχεύσεις RP
⸀ • **φονεύσῃς** WH Treg NA28] φονεύσεις RP
⸂ • **μοιχεύεις φονεύεις** WH Treg NA28] μοιχεύσεις φονεύσεις RP
⸃ • **μοιχεύεις φονεύεις** WH Treg NA28] μοιχεύσεις φονεύσεις RP
⸀ **13 ἔλεος** WH Treg NA28] ἔλεον RP
⸀ **14 Τί** WH] + τὸ Treg NA28 RP
⸀ **15 ἐὰν** WH Treg NA28] + δὲ RP
⸀ • **λειπόμενοι** WH Treg NA27] + ὦσιν NA28 RP

⸀16 **τί** WH] + τὸ Treg NA28 RP
⸂17 **ἔχῃ ἔργα** WH Treg NA28] ἔργα ἔχῃ RP
⸃17 **ἔχῃ ἔργα** WH Treg NA28] ἔργα ἔχῃ RP
⸀18 **χωρὶς** WH Treg NA28] ἐκ RP
⸀ • **ἔργων** WH Treg NA28] + σου RP
⸂ • **σοι δείξω** WH Treg NA28] δείξω σοι RP
⸃ • **σοι δείξω** WH Treg NA28] δείξω σοι RP
⸀ • **πίστιν** WH Treg NA28] + μου RP
⸂19 **εἷς ἐστιν ὁ θεός** Treg NA28] εἷς θεός ἐστιν WH; ὁ θεὸς εἷς ἐστιν RP
⸃19 **εἷς ἐστιν ὁ θεός** Treg NA28] εἷς θεός ἐστιν WH; ὁ θεὸς εἷς ἐστιν RP
⸀20 **ἀργή** WH Treg NA28] νεκρά RP
⸀24 **ὁρᾶτε** WH Treg NA28] + τοίνυν RP
⸀26 **γὰρ** Treg NA28 RP] – WH
⸀ • **χωρὶς** WH NA28] + τῶν Treg RP

JAMES 3

⸂3:3 **εἰ δὲ** WH Treg NA28] Ἴδε RP
⸃3:3 **εἰ δὲ** WH Treg NA28] Ἴδε RP
⸀ • **εἰς** WH Treg NA28] πρὸς RP
⸂4 **ἀνέμων σκληρῶν** WH Treg NA28] σκληρῶν ἀνέμων RP
⸃4 **ἀνέμων σκληρῶν** WH Treg NA28] σκληρῶν ἀνέμων RP
⸂ • **ἡ … βούλεται** WH Treg NA28] ἂν ἡ … βούληται RP
⸃ • **ἡ … βούλεται** WH Treg NA28] ἂν ἡ … βούληται RP
⸂5 **μεγάλα αὐχεῖ** WH Treg NA28] μεγαλαυχεῖ RP
⸃5 **μεγάλα αὐχεῖ** WH Treg NA28] μεγαλαυχεῖ RP
⸀ • **ἡλίκον** WH Treg NA28] ὀλίγον RP
⸀6 **ἀδικίας** WH Treg NA28] + οὕτως RP
⸂8 **δαμάσαι δύναται ἀνθρώπων** WH Treg NA28] δύναται ἀνθρώπων δαμάσαι RP
⸃8 **δαμάσαι δύναται ἀνθρώπων** WH Treg NA28] δύναται ἀνθρώπων δαμάσαι RP
⸀ • **ἀκατάστατον** WH Treg NA28] ἀκατάσχετον RP
⸀9 **κύριον** WH Treg NA28] θεὸν RP
⸂12 **οὔτε ἁλυκὸν** WH Treg NA28] Οὕτως οὐδεμια πηγὴ ἁλυκὸν καὶ RP
⸃12 **οὔτε ἁλυκὸν** WH Treg NA28] Οὕτως οὐδεμια πηγὴ ἁλυκὸν καὶ RP

⸀**17 ἀδιάκριτος** WH Treg NA28] + καὶ RP
⸀**18 δὲ** WH Treg NA28] + τῆς RP

JAMES 4

⸀**4:1 πόθεν** WH Treg NA28] – RP
⸀**4 μοιχαλίδες** WH Treg NA28] Μοιχοὶ καὶ μοιχαλίδες RP
⸀ • **ἐὰν** WH NA28] ἂν Treg RP
⸀**5 κατῴκισεν** WH Treg NA28] κατῴκησεν RP
⸀**8 ἐγγιεῖ** Treg NA28 RP] ἐγγίσει WH
⸀**9 μετατραπήτω** WH NA28] μεταστραφήτω Treg RP
⸀**10 κυρίου** WH Treg NA27] τοῦ κυρίου NA28 RP
⸀**11 ἢ** WH Treg NA28] καὶ RP
⸀**12 ἐστιν** WH] + ὁ Treg NA28 RP
⸂ • **καὶ κριτής** WH Treg NA28] – RP
⸃ • **καὶ κριτής** WH Treg NA28] – RP
⸂ • **ὁ κρίνων** WH Treg NA28] ὃς κρίνεις RP
⸃ • **ὁ κρίνων** WH Treg NA28] ὃς κρίνεις RP
⸀ • **πλησίον** WH Treg NA28] ἕτερον RP
⸀**13 ἢ** WH Treg NA28] καὶ RP
⸀ • **πορευσόμεθα** WH Treg NA28] πορευσώμεθα RP
⸀ • **ποιήσομεν** WH NA28] ποιήσωμεν Treg RP
⸀ • **ἐνιαυτὸν** WH Treg NA28] + ἕνα RP
⸀ • **ἐμπορευσόμεθα** WH Treg NA28] ἐμπορευσώμεθα RP
⸀ • **κερδήσομεν** WH Treg NA28] κερδήσωμεν RP
⸀**14 τὸ** Treg NA28 RP] – WH
⸀ • **ποία** WH NA28] + γὰρ Treg RP
⸀ • **ἐστε** WH Treg NA28] ἔσται RP
⸀ • **ἡ** Treg NA28 RP] – WH
⸀ • **ἔπειτα** WH Treg NA28] + δὲ RP
⸀**15 θελήσῃ** Treg NA28 RP] θέλῃ WH
⸀ • **ζήσομεν** WH Treg NA28] ζήσωμεν RP
⸀ • **ποιήσομεν** WH Treg NA28] ποιήσωμεν RP

JAMES 5

⸀**5:4 ἀφυστερημένος** WH Treg] ἀπεστερημένος NA28 RP
⸀ • **εἰσεληλύθασιν** NA28 RP] εἰσελήλυθαν WH Treg
⸀**5 ὑμῶν** WH Treg NA28] + ὡς RP
⸀**7 αὐτῷ** WH Treg NA28] αὐτόν RP

⸀ • **λάβῃ** WH Treg NA28] + ὑετὸν RP

⸂ 9 **ἀδελφοί κατ' ἀλλήλων** WH Treg NA28] κατ' ἀλλήλων ἀδελφοί RP

⸃ 9 **ἀδελφοί κατ' ἀλλήλων** WH Treg NA28] κατ' ἀλλήλων ἀδελφοί RP

⸀ 10 **ἀδελφοί** WH Treg NA28] + μου RP

⸀ • **ἐν** WH Treg NA28] – RP

⸀ 11 **ὑπομείναντας** WH Treg NA28] ὑπομένοντας RP

⸀ • **εἴδετε** WH Treg NA28] ἴδετε RP

⸂ • **ὁ κύριος** WH Treg NA28] – RP

⸃ • **ὁ κύριος** WH Treg NA28] – RP

⸂ 12 **ὑπὸ κρίσιν** WH Treg NA28] εἰς ὑπὸκρίσιν RP

⸃ 12 **ὑπὸ κρίσιν** WH Treg NA28] εἰς ὑπὸκρίσιν RP

⸀ 14 **αὐτὸν** Treg NA28 RP] – WH

⸀ 16 **οὖν** WH Treg NA28] – RP

⸂ • **τὰς ἁμαρτίας** WH Treg NA28] τὰ παραπτώματα RP

⸃ • **τὰς ἁμαρτίας** WH Treg NA28] τὰ παραπτώματα RP

⸀ • **εὔχεσθε** Treg NA28 RP] προσεύχεσθε WH

⸂ 18 **ὑετὸν ἔδωκεν** WH NA28 RP] ἔδωκεν ὑετὸν Treg

⸃ 18 **ὑετὸν ἔδωκεν** WH NA28 RP] ἔδωκεν ὑετὸν Treg

⸀ 19 **μου** WH Treg NA28] – RP

⸀ 20 **γινωσκέτω** Treg NA28 RP] γινώσκετε WH

⸀ • **αὐτοῦ** WH NA28] – Treg RP

The SBLGNT in Comparison to ECM

In the Catholic letters, the SBLGNT differs from the ECM at thirty-nine places, five of which are in James and are listed below.

Ref.	SBLGNT] ECM
James	
2:4	οὐ διεκρίθητε] καὶ οὐ διεκρίθητε
2:14	Τί ὄφελος] Τί τὸ ὄφελος
2:16	Τί ὄφελος] Τί τὸ ὄφελος
4:12	νομοθέτης] •ὁ• νομοθέτης
5:4	ἀφυστερημένος] ἀπεστερημένος

Appendix II

VOCABULARY 50 TIMES OF MORE SORTED BY FREQUENCY

19796	ὁ, ἡ, τό	*the; (sub.) he, she, thing*
8984	καί	*and; (adv.) also, even*
5569	αὐτός, ή, ό	*he, she, it; (adj.) -self, same*
2899	σύ, σοῦ; ὑμεῖς, ὑμῶν	*you; you all*
2777	δέ	*but, rather, and, now*
2737	ἐν	*(+dat) in, with, among*
2582	ἐγώ, (ἐ)μοῦ; ἡμεῖς, ἡμῶν	*I; we*
2458	εἰμί	*I am, exist, happen*
2352	λέγω	*I say, speak, claim*
1857	εἰς	*(+acc) to, into*
1621	οὐ, οὐκ, οὐχ	*not, no*
1407	ὅς, ἥ, ὅ	*who, which, that*
1387	οὗτος, αὕτη, τοῦτο	*this; (sub.) he, she, this one*
1307	θεός, οῦ, ὁ and ἡ	*God, god, divine one*
1294	ὅτι	*that, because*
1243	πᾶς, πᾶσα, πᾶν	*every, each, all, whole*
1039	γάρ	*for, because, since*
1038	μή	*not, no; (+subj.) in order that...not*
913	ἐκ, ἐξ	*(+gen) from, out from*
911	Ἰησοῦς, οῦ, ὁ	*Joshua, Jesus*
887	ἐπί	*(+gen/dat/acc) on, near, toward*
714	κύριος, ου, ὁ	*Lord, master, owner*
707	ἔχω	*I have, am*
698	πρός	*(+acc) to, toward, with*
667	γίνομαι	*I am, become, happen*
666	διά	*(+gen) through; (+acc) because of*
663	ἵνα	*in order that, so that*

645	ἀπό	*(+gen) from, away from*
638	ἀλλά	*but, yet, rather*
633	ἔρχομαι	*I come, go*
568	ποιέω	*I make, do*
551	τίς, τί	*who? which? what?*
550	ἄνθρωπος, ου, ὁ	*man, human*
534	τις, τι	*someone, something*
528	Χριστός, οῦ, ὁ	*Messiah, Anointed One, Christ*
504	ὡς	*as, like*
502	εἰ	*if, whether*
495	οὖν	*therefore, then*
470	κατά	*(+gen) against, down; (+acc) according to*
470	μετά	*(+gen) with; (+acc) after, behind*
453	ὁράω	*I see, perceive, experience*
428	ἀκούω	*I hear, obey, listen*
415	πολύς, πολλή, πολύ	*much, many*
415	δίδωμι	*I give, entrust*
413	πατήρ, πατρός, ὁ	*father*
389	ἡμέρα, ας, ἡ	*day, time*
379	πνεῦμα, ατος, τό	*spirit, breath*
375	υἱός, οῦ, ὁ	*son*
346	ἤ	*or, than*
344	εἷς, μία, ἕν	*one, single*
342	ἀδελφός , οῦ, ὁ	*brother*
332	περί	*(+gen) concerning; (+acc) around*
330	ἐάν	*if, whenever*
330	λόγος, ου, ὁ	*word, speech, matter*
321	ἑαυτοῦ, ῆς, οῦ	*himself, herself, itself*
320	οἶδα	*I know, understand*
297	λαλέω	*I speak*
273	οὐρανός, οῦ, ὁ	*sky, heaven*
262	μαθητής, οῦ, ὁ	*disciple, student*

258	λαμβάνω	*I take, receive*
250	γῆ, γῆς, ἡ	*land, earth*
243	ἐκεῖνος, η, ο	*that; (sub.) he, she, that one*
243	μέγας, μεγάλη, μέγα	*large, great*
242	πίστις, εως, ἡ	*belief, faithfulness, trust, fidelity, faith*
241	πιστεύω	*I believe, trust*
233	ἅγιος, ία, ον	*holy, pure, devout; (sub.) Saint*
232	ἀποκρίνομαι	*I answer*
229	ὄνομα, ατος, τό	*name*
227	οὐδείς, οὐδεμία, οὐδέν	*no; (sub.) no one, nothing*
221	γινώσκω	*I know, understand, learn*
221	ὑπό	*(+gen) by; (+acc) underneath*
217	ἐξέρχομαι	*I go out, exit*
216	ἀνήρ, ἀνδρός, ὁ	*man, husband*
216	γυνή, αικός, ἡ	*woman, wife*
213	τέ	*and, so*
209	δύναμαι	*I am able*
208	θέλω	*I wish, want*
207	οὕτω/οὕτως	*thus, so*
200	ἰδού	*Look!, Notice!, See!*
195	Ἰουδαῖος, αία, αῖον	*Jewish; (sub.) Jew*
194	νόμος, ου, ὁ	*law, custom*
193	εἰσέρχομαι	*I go into, enter*
193	παρά	*(+gen) along side, from; (+dat) beside, near; (+acc) out from, by*
192	γράφω	*I write*
185	κόσμος, ου, ὁ	*world, universe, order*
182	καθώς	*as, just as*
178	μέν	*however, but, indeed*
176	χείρ, χειρός, ἡ	*hand*
176	εὑρίσκω	*I find, discover*

175	ἄγγελος, ου, ὁ	*messenger, envoy, angel*
174	ὄχλος, ου, ὁ	*crowd, multitude*
172	ἁμαρτία, ίας, ἡ	*sin, guilt, failure*
170	ἄν	*ever [conditional particle, indicates possibility]*
169	ἔργον, ου, τό	*work, accomplishment*
165	δόξα, ης, ἡ	*splendor, glory; reputation*
163	πόλις, εως, ἡ	*town, city*
162	βασιλεία, ας, ἡ	*kingdom, providence, dominion*
160	ἔθνος, ους, τό	*nation, culture group, people*
159	τότε	*at that time, then*
158	ἐσθίω	*I eat, drink, consume*
158	Παῦλος, ου, ὁ	*Paul*
156	καρδία, ας, ἡ	*heart*
156	Πέτρος, ου, ὁ	*Peter*
155	πρῶτος, η, ον	*first, most prominent*
155	χάρις, ιτος, ἡ	*grace, thankfulness, kindness*
154	ἄλλος, η, ο	*other, another*
154	ἵστημι	*I set, place, establish*
153	πορεύομαι	*I go, walk*
150	ὑπέρ	*(+gen) on behalf of, for; (+acc) over, beyond*
148	καλέω	*I call, summon, invite*
147	σάρξ, σαρκός, ἡ	*flesh, muscle, body*
145	νῦν	*now, currently, presently*
145	ἕως	*while, until, up to the point of, as far as*
144	ὅστις, ἥτις, ὅ τι	*whoever, whichever, any one who*
144	προφήτης, ου, ὁ	*prophet*
143	ἐγείρω	*I rise, raise*
143	ἀγαπάω	*I love, adore*

143 ἀφίημι — *I release, forgive, reprieve; depart*
143 οὐδέ — *but not, nor, neither*
142 λαός, οῦ, ὁ — *people, populace, multitude*
142 σῶμα, ατος, τό — *body*
141 πάλιν — *again*
140 ζάω — *I live*
139 φωνή, ῆς, ἡ — *voice, sound, communication*
135 δύο — *two*
135 ζωή, ῆς, ἡ — *life, existence*
135 Ἰωάν(ν)ης, ου, ὁ — *John*
133 βλέπω — *I see, observe, notice*
131 ἀποστέλλω — *I send (off)*
129 σύν — *(+dat) with, along with*
128 ἀμήν — *certainly, truly, indeed*
128 νεκρός, ά, όν — *dead*
126 δοῦλος, ου, ὁ — *slave, bondservant*
123 ὅταν — *whenever, when*
122 αἰών, ῶνος, ὁ — *age, era, lifetime*
122 ἀρχιερεύς, έως, ὁ — *high priest, chief priest*
122 βάλλω — *I throw, place*
120 θάνατος, ου, ὁ — *death*
119 δύναμις, εως, ἡ — *power, strength, ability*
119 παραδίδωμι — *I hand over, deliver, grant*
118 μένω — *I remain, continue*
117 ἀπέρχομαι — *I depart, go away*
117 ζητέω — *I seek, search, inquire*
116 ἀγάπη, ης, ἡ — *love, adoration*
115 βασιλεύς, έως, ὁ — *king*
115 κρίνω — *I judge, decide, choose*
114 ἐκκλησία, ας, ἡ — *assembly, gathering, community, church*
114 ἴδιος, ία, ον — *one's own*
113 μόνος, η, ον — *alone, only*

113	οἶκος, ου, ὁ	*house, dwelling, family*
111	ἀποθνῄσκω	*I die, perish*
111	ὅσος, η, ον	*as many as, as much as, as great as*
109	ἀλήθεια, ας, ἡ	*truth, reality*
109	μέλλω	*I am about to, intend*
109	παρακαλέω	*I encourage, call, request*
108	ὅλος, η, ον	*whole, entire*
108	ἀνίστημι	*I raise, resurrect, establish*
106	σῴζω	*I save, rescue, keep safe*
106	ὥρα, ας, ἡ	*hour, time, period, season*
105	πῶς	*how?*
102	ὅτε	*when*
102	ψυχή, ῆς, ἡ	*soul, life*
102	ἐξουσία, ας, ἡ	*authority, capability*
101	ἀγαθός, ή, όν	*good, beneficial*
101	αἴρω	*I lift up, raise up, take away*
101	δεῖ	*I must, am required, ought*
101	ὁδός, οῦ, ἡ	*road, way, path, trip*
101	καλός, ή, όν	*beautiful, good, noble*
100	ἀλλήλων	*one another*
100	ὀφθαλμός, οῦ,	*eye*
100	τίθημι	*I put, place, lay*
99	τέκνον, ου, τό	*child*
97	ἕτερος, α, ον	*other, another*
97	Φαρισαῖος, ου, ὁ	*Pharisee, Separatist*
97	αἷμα, ατος, τό	*blood, bloodshed*
97	ἄρτος, ου, ὁ	*bread, food*
97	γεννάω	*I beget, give birth, parent*
97	διδάσκω	*I teach, instruct*
95	ἐκεῖ	*there*
95	περιπατέω	*I walk (about), live, behave*

95	φοβέω	*I fear, respect; I flee frightened*
94	ἐνώπιον	*before, face to face, in the view of*
94	τόπος, ου, ὁ	*place, position*
93	ἔτι	*yet, still, even now*
93	οἰκία, ας, ἡ	*house, building, family*
93	πούς, ποδός, ὁ	*foot*
91	δικαιοσύνη, ης, ἡ	*righteousness, justice*
91	εἰρήνη, ης, ἡ	*peace, well-being*
91	θάλασσα, ης, ἡ	*lake, sea*
91	κάθημαι	*I sit, settle, reside*
91	μηδείς, μηδεμία, μηδέν	*no, no one, nothing*
90	ἀπόλλυμι	*ruin, destroy, perish*
90	πίπτω	*I fall, collapse*
89	ἀκολουθέω	*I follow, obey*
88	ἑπτά	*seven*
87	οὔτε	*and not, nor, neither*
86	ἄρχω	*I rule, lead, begin*
86	πληρόω	*I fill, complete, fulfill*
85	προσέρχομαι	*I go to, visit, approach*
85	καιρός, οῦ, ὁ	*time, period, season*
85	προσεύχομαι	*I pray, petition a deity*
83	κἀγώ	*and I, I too (crasis καὶ ἐγώ)*
83	μήτηρ, τρός, ἡ	*mother*
83	ὥστε	*so that, therefore, consequently*
82	ἕκαστος, η, ον	*every, each*
81	ἀναβαίνω	*I go up, ascend*
81	ὅπου	*where, whereas, whenever*
81	ἐκβάλλω	*I throw out, expel, reject*
81	μᾶλλον	*more, exceedingly, rather*
80	καταβαίνω	*I go down, descend*
80	Μωϋσῆς, ὁ	*Moses*

79	ἀπόστολος, ου, ὁ	*delegate, ambassador, apostle*
79	δίκαιος, αία, ον	*just, righteous, fair*
79	πέμπω	*I send, despatch*
79	ὑπάγω	*I withdraw, go away*
78	πονηρός, ά, όν	*evil, bad, worthless, sick*
78	στόμα, ατος, τό	*mouth, opening*
77	ἀνοίγω	*I open*
77	βαπτίζω	*I soak, submerge, wash, baptize*
77	Ἰερουσαλήμ, ἡ	*Jerusalem*
77	σημεῖον, ου, τό	*sign, mark, signal, miracle*
76	μαρτυρέω	*I give evidence, witness, testify*
76	πρόσωπον, ου, τό	*face, appearance, expression, presence*
76	ὕδωρ, ατος, τό	*water, rain*
75	εὐαγγέλιον, ου, τό	*good news, gospel*
75	δώδεκα	*twelve*
75	κεφαλή, ῆς, ἡ	*head*
75	Σίμων, ωνος, ὁ	*Simon*
74	ἀποκτείνω, ἀποκτέννω	*I kill, slay*
74	χαίρω	*I am glad, rejoice, welcome*
73	Ἀβραάμ, ὁ	*Abraham*
72	πίνω	*I drink*
72	φῶς, φωτός, τό	*light, torch*
72	ἱερόν, οῦ, τό	*temple, holy place*
71	πῦρ, ός, τό	*fire*
71	τηρέω	*I watch over, guard, keep*
70	αἰτέω	*I ask, demand*
69	αἰώνιος, ον	*long-lasting, eternal*
69	ἄγω	*I lead, carry, arrest, observe*
68	ἐμός, ή, όν	*my, mine*
68	τρεῖς, τρία	*three*

68	Ἰσραήλ, ὁ	*Israel*
68	σάββατον, ου, τό	*Sabbath*
67	ῥῆμα, ατος, τό	*word, saying, thing*
67	πιστός, ή, όν	*faithful, trustworthy, believing*
67	πλοῖον, ου, τό	*boat, ship, vessel*
67	ἀπολύω	*I release, pardon, dismiss*
66	ἐντολή, ῆς, ἡ	*command, order, commandment*
66	κάρπος, ου, ὁ	*fruit, produce, profit*
66	πρεσβύτερος, α, ον	*aged, old;* (Subst.) *elder*
66	φέρω	*I carry, bring, lead*
65	φημί	*I say, declare*
65	εἴτε	*if, either, or, whether*
63	γραμματεύς, έως, ὁ	*scribe, law expert, high official*
63	δαιμόνιον, ου, τό	*demon, evil spirit, inferior divinity*
63	ἐρωτάω	*I ask, inquire, question*
63	ὄρος, ους, τό	*mountain, hill*
62	ἔξω	*outside, out*
62	δοκέω	*I think, suppose, form an opinion; I seem, suppose*
62	θέλημα, ατος, τό	*will, want*
62	θρόνος, ου, ὁ	*chair, seat, throne*
62	Ἱεροσόλυμα, τά	*Jerusalem (city or its inhabitants)*
61	ἀγαπητός, ή, όν	*beloved, dearly loved*
61	Γαλιλαία, ας, ἡ	*Galilee*
61	δοξάζω	*I honor, esteem in high regard, exalt, glorify*
61	κηρύσσω	*I preach, proclaim, announce*
61	νύξ, νυκτός, ἡ	*night (often metaph.)*
61	ὧδε	*here, thus, in this way, exceedingly so*

60	ἤδη	*already, now; by this time*
60	ἱμάτιον, ου, τό	*garment; outer garment*
60	προσκυνέω	*I worship, prostrate myself*
60	ὑπάρχω	*I am present, at one's disposal; I am, exist*
59	ἀσπάζομαι	*I greet, welcome*
59	Δαυίδ, ὁ	*David*
59	διδάσκαλος, ου, ὁ	*teacher, master*
59	λίθος, ου, ὁ	*stone*
59	συνάγω	*I gather together, collect; receive as a guest*
59	χαρά, ᾶς, ἡ	*joy, delight, gladness*
59	εὐθύς, εῖα, ύ	*immediately, straight, proper*
58	θεωρέω	*I view (as a spectator), behold, observe, see*
58	μέσος, η, ον	*middle, in the midst*
57	τοιοῦτος, αύτη, οῦτον	*such as this, of such a kind*
56	δέχομαι	*I take, receive; welcome*
56	ἐπερωτάω	*I ask, inquire*
56	μηδέ	*but not, nor; not even, not either*
56	συναγωγή, ῆς, ἡ	*assembly, gathering; synagogue*
56	τρίτος, η, ον	*third*
55	ἀρχή, ῆς, ἡ	*beginning; power; rule*
55	κράζω	*I call out, cry out, scream*
55	λοιπός, ή, όν	*rest, remaining; from now on*
55	Πιλᾶτος, ου, ὁ	*Pilate*
54	δεξιός, ά, όν	*right (directional; often metph.); true*
54	εὐαγγελίζω	*I bring/proclaim (the) good news*

54	οὐχί	*not, no, in no way (intensified οὐ)*
53	χρόνος, ου, ὁ	*time, occasion*
53	διό	*therefore, for this reason*
53	ἐλπίς, ίδος, ἡ	*expectation, hope*
53	ὅπως	*how; in order that*
52	ἐπαγγελία, ας, ἡ	*promise, offer*
52	ἔσχατος, η, ον	*last, farthest, least*
52	παιδίον, ου, τό	*child; young servant/slave*
52	πείθω	*I persuade, win over; depend on*
52	σπείρω	*I sow seed, scatter*
51	σοφία, ας, ἡ	*wisdom, sound judgement*
50	γλῶσσα, ης, ἡ	*tongue; language; joyful speech*
50	κακός, ή, όν	*evil, bad; incorrect*
50	μακάριος, ία, ιον	*favored, blessed*
50	παραβολή, ῆς, ἡ	*parable, illustration; type, embodiment*
50	τυφλός, ή, όν	*blind (often metaph.)*
49	γραφή, ῆς, ἡ	*scripture, writing*[1]

1 Though γραγή occurs 49 times in the SBLGNT, this word occurs 50 times in the NA. As such, many resources include γραφή in their most frequently occurring word list and retention requirements. To retain this standard, it has also been included in this most frequently occurring vocabulary list. Γραγή is not included in the General Reader's footnotes or chapter vocabulary helps.

Appendix III

VOCABULARY 50 TIMES OF MORE ARRANGED ALPHABETICALLY

Α α

Ἀβραάμ, ὁ	*Abraham*
ἀγαθός, ή, όν	*good, beneficial*
ἀγαπάω	*I love, adore*
ἀγάπη, ης, ἡ	*love, adoration*
ἀγαπητός, ή, όν	*beloved, dearly loved*
ἄγγελος, ου, ὁ	*messenger, envoy, angel*
ἅγιος, ία, ον	*holy, pure, devout; (Subst.) Saint*
ἄγω	*I lead, carry, arrest, observe*
ἀδελφός , οῦ, ὁ	*brother*
αἷμα, ατος, τό	*blood, bloodshed*
αἴρω	*I lift up, raise up, take away*
αἰτέω	*I ask, demand*
αἰών, ῶνος, ὁ	*age, era, lifetime*
αἰώνιος, ον	*long-lasting, eternal*
ἀκολουθέω	*I follow, obey*
ἀκούω	*I hear, obey, listen*
ἀλήθεια, ας, ἡ	*truth, reality*
ἀλλά	*but, yet, rather*
ἀλλήλων	*one another*
ἄλλος, η, ο	*other, another*
ἁμαρτία, ίας, ἡ	*sin, guilt, failure*
ἀμήν	*certainly, truly, indeed*
ἄν	*ever [conditional particle, indicates possibility]*
ἀναβαίνω	*I go up, ascend*
ἀνήρ, ἀνδρός, ὁ	*man, husband*
ἄνθρωπος, ου, ὁ	*man, human*
ἀνίστημι	*I raise, resurrect, establish*
ἀνοίγω	*I open*
ἀπέρχομαι	*I depart, go away*

VOCABULARY 50 TIMES OR MORE ARRANGED ALPHABETICALLY

ἀπό	*(+gen) from, away from*
ἀποθνῄσκω	*I die, perish*
ἀποκρίνομαι	*I answer*
ἀποκτείνω, ἀποκτέννω	*I kill, slay*
ἀπόλλυμι	*I ruin, destroy, perish*
ἀπολύω	*I release, pardon, dismiss*
ἀποστέλλω	*I send (off)*
ἀπόστολος, ου, ὁ	*delegate, ambassador, apostle*
ἄρτος, ου, ὁ	*bread, food*
ἀρχή, ῆς, ἡ	*beginning; power; rule*
ἀρχιερεύς, έως, ὁ	*high priest, chief priest*
ἄρχω	*I rule, lead, begin*
ἀσπάζομαι	*I greet, welcome*
αὐτός, ή, ό	*he, she, it; (adj.) -self, same*
ἀφίημι	*I release, forgive, reprieve; depart*

Β β

βάλλω	*I throw, place*
βαπτίζω	*I soak, submerge, wash, baptize*
βασιλεία, ας, ἡ	*kingdom, providence, dominion*
βασιλεύς, έως, ὁ	*king*
βλέπω	*I see, observe, notice*

Γ γ

Γαλιλαία, ας, ἡ	*Galilee*
γάρ	*for, because, since*
γεννάω	*I beget, give birth, parent*
γῆ, γῆς, ἡ	*land, earth*
γίνομαι	*I am, become, happen*
γινώσκω	*I know, understand, learn*
γλῶσσα, ης, ἡ	*tongue; language; joyful speech*
γραμματεύς, έως, ὁ	*scribe, law expert, high official*
γραφή, ῆς, ἡ	*scripture, writing*

γράφω	*I write*
γυνή, αικός, ἡ	*woman, wife*

Δ δ

δαιμόνιον, ου, τό	*demon, evil spirit, inferior divinity*
Δαυίδ, ὁ	*David*
δέ	*but, rather, and, now*
δεῖ	*I must, am required, ought*
δεξιός, ά, όν	*right (directional; often metph.); true*
δέχομαι	*I take, receive; welcome*
διά	*(+gen) through; (+acc) because of*
διδάσκαλος, ου, ὁ	*teacher, master*
διδάσκω	*I teach, instruct*
δίδωμι	*I give, entrust*
δίκαιος, αία, ον	*just, righteous, fair*
δικαιοσύνη, ης, ἡ	*righteousness, justice*
διό	*therefore, for this reason*
δοκέω	*I think, suppose, form an opinion; I seem, suppose*
δόξα, ης, ἡ	*splendor, glory; reputation*
δοξάζω	*I honor, esteem in high regard, exalt, glorify*
δοῦλος, ου, ὁ	*slave, bondservant*
δύναμαι	*I am able*
δύναμις, εως, ἡ	*power, strength, ability*
δύο	*two*
δώδεκα	*twelve*

Ε ε

ἐάν	*if, whenever*
ἑαυτοῦ, ῆς, οῦ	*himself, herself, itself*
ἐγείρω	*I rise, raise*

ἐγώ, (ἐ)μοῦ; ἡμεῖς, ἡμῶν	*I; we*
ἔθνος, ους, τό	*nation, culture group, people*
εἰ	*if, whether*
εἰμί	*I am, exist, happen*
εἰρήνη, ης, ἡ	*peace, well-being*
εἷς, μία, ἕν	*one, single*
εἰς	*(+acc) to, into*
εἰσέρχομαι	*I go into, enter*
εἴτε	*if, either, or, whether*
ἐκ, ἐξ	*(+gen) from, out from*
ἕκαστος, η, ον	*every, each*
ἐκβάλλω	*I throw out, expel, reject*
ἐκεῖ	*there*
ἐκεῖνος, η, ο	*that; (Subst.) he, she, that one*
ἐκκλησία, ας, ἡ	*assembly, gathering, community, church*
ἐλπίς, ίδος, ἡ	*expectation, hope*
ἐμός, ή, όν	*my, mine*
ἐν	*(+dat) in, with, among*
ἐντολή, ῆς, ἡ	*command, order, commandment*
ἐνώπιον	*before, face to face, in the view of*
ἐξέρχομαι	*I go out, exit*
ἐξουσία, ας, ἡ	*authority, capability*
ἔξω	*outside, out*
ἐπαγγελία, ας, ἡ	*promise, offer*
ἐπερωτάω	*I ask, inquire*
ἐπί	*(+gen/dat/acc) on, near, toward*
ἑπτά	*seven*
ἔργον, ου, τό	*work, accomplishment*
ἔρχομαι	*I come, go*
ἐρωτάω	*I ask, inquire, question*
ἐσθίω	*I eat, drink, consume*
ἔσχατος, η, ον	*last, farthest, least*
ἕτερος, α, ον	*other, another*
ἔτι	*yet, still, even now*
εὐαγγελίζω	*I bring/proclaim (the) good news*
εὐαγγέλιον, ου, τό	*good news, gospel*

εὐθύς, εῖα, ύ	*immediately, straight, proper*
εὑρίσκω	*I find, discover*
ἔχω	*I have, am*
ἕως	*while, until, up to the point of, as far as*

Ζ ζ

ζάω	*I live*
ζητέω	*I seek, search, inquire*
ζωή, ῆς, ἡ	*life, existence*

Η η

ἤ	*or, than*
ἤδη	*already, now; by this time*
ἡμέρα, ας, ἡ	*day, time*

Θ ϑ

ϑάλασσα, ης, ἡ	*lake, sea*
ϑάνατος, ου, ὁ	*death*
ϑέλημα, ατος, τό	*will, want*
ϑέλω	*I wish, want*
ϑεός, οῦ, ὁ and ἡ	*God, god, divine one*
ϑεωρέω	*I view (as a spectator), behold, observe, see*
ϑρόνος, ου, ὁ	*chair, seat, throne*

Ι ι

ἴδιος, ία, ον	*one's own*
ἰδού	*Look!, Notice!, See!*

ἱερόν, οῦ, τό — *temple, holy place*
Ἱεροσόλυμα, τά — *Jerusalem (city or its inhabitants)*
Ἰερουσαλήμ, ἡ — *Jerusalem*
Ἰησοῦς, οῦ, ὁ — *Joshua, Jesus*
ἱμάτιον, ου, τό — *garment; outer garment*
ἵνα — *in order that, so that*
Ἰουδαῖος, αία, αῖον — *Jewish; (Subst..) Jew*
Ἰσραήλ, ὁ — *Israel*
ἵστημι — *I set, place, establish*
Ἰωάν(ν)ης, ου, ὁ — *John*

Κ κ

κἀγώ — *and I, I too (crasis καὶ ἐγώ)*
κάθημαι — *I sit, settle, reside*
καθώς — *as, just as*
καί — *and; (adv.) also, even*
καιρός, οῦ, ὁ — *time, period, season*
κακός, ή, όν — *evil, bad; incorrect*
καλέω — *I call, summon, invite*
καλός, ή, όν — *beautiful, good, noble*
καρδία, ας, ἡ — *heart*
κάρπος, ου, ὁ — *fruit, produce, profit*
κατά — *(+gen) against, down; (+acc) according to*
καταβαίνω — *I go down, descend*
κεφαλή, ῆς, ἡ — *head*
κηρύσσω — *I preach, proclaim, announce*
κόσμος, ου, ὁ — *world, universe, order*
κράζω — *I call out, cry out, scream*
κρίνω — *I judge, decide, choose*
κύριος, ου, ὁ — *Lord, master, owner*

Λ λ

λαλέω	*I speak*
λαμβάνω	*I take, receive*
λαός, οῦ, ὁ	*people, populace, multitude*
λέγω	*I say, speak, claim*
λίθος, ου, ὁ	*stone*
λόγος, ου, ὁ	*word, speech, matter*
λοιπός, ή, όν	*rest, remaining; from now on*

Μ μ

μαθητής, οῦ, ὁ	*disciple, student*
μακάριος, ία, ιον	*favored, blessed*
μᾶλλον	*more, exceedingly, rather*
μαρτυρέω	*I give evidence, witness, testify*
μέγας, μεγάλη, μέγα	*large, great*
μέλλω	*I am about to, intend*
μέν	*however, but, indeed*
μένω	*I remain, continue*
μέσος, η, ον	*middle, in the midst*
μετά	*(+gen) with; (+acc) after, behind*
μή	*not, no; (+subj.) in order that…not*
μηδέ	*but not, nor; not even, not either*
μηδείς, μηδεμία, μηδέν	*no, no one, nothing*
μήτηρ, τρός, ἡ	*mother*
μόνος, η, ον	*alone, only*
Μωϋσῆς, ὁ	*Moses*

Ν ν

νεκρός, ά, όν	*dead*
νόμος, ου, ὁ	*law, custom*
νῦν	*now, currently, presently*
νύξ, νυκτός, ἡ	*night (often metaph.)*

Ο ο

ὁ, ἡ, τό	*the; (Subst.) he, she, thing*
ὁδός, οῦ, ἡ	*road, way, path, trip*
οἶδα	*I know, understand*
οἰκία, ας, ἡ	*house, building, family*
οἶκος, ου, ὁ	*house, dwelling, family*
ὅλος, η, ον	*whole, entire*
ὄνομα, ατος, τό	*name*
ὅπου	*where, whereas, whenever*
ὅπως	*how; in order that*
ὁράω	*I see, perceive, experience*
ὄρος, ους, τό	*mountain, hill*
ὅς, ἥ, ὅ	*who, which, that*
ὅσος, η, ον	*as many as, as much as, as great as*
ὅστις, ἥτις, ὅ τι	*whoever, whichever, any one who*
ὅταν	*whenever, when*
ὅτε	*when*
ὅτι	*that, because*
οὐ, οὐκ, οὐχ	*not, no*
οὐδέ	*but not, nor, neither*
οὐδείς, οὐδεμία, οὐδέν	*no; (Subst.) no one, nothing*
οὖν	*therefore, then*
οὐρανός, οῦ, ὁ	*sky, heaven*
οὔτε	*and not, nor, neither*
οὗτος, αὕτη, τοῦτο	*this; (Subst.) he, she, this one*
οὕτω/οὕτως	*thus, so*
οὐχί	*not, no, in no way (intensified οὐ)*
ὀφθαλμός, οῦ,	*eye*
ὄχλος, ου, ὁ	*crowd, multitude*

Π π

παιδίον, ου, τό	*child; young servant/slave*
πάλιν	*again*

παρά	*(+gen) along side, from; (+dat) beside, near; (+acc) out from, by*
παραβολή, ῆς, ἡ	*parable, illustration; type, embodiment*
παραδίδωμι	*I hand over, deliver, grant*
παρακαλέω	*I encourage, call, request*
πᾶς, πᾶσα, πᾶν	*every, each, all, whole*
πατήρ, πατρός, ὁ	*father*
Παῦλος, ου, ὁ	*Paul*
πείθω	*I persuade, win over; depend on*
πέμπω	*I send, despatch*
περί	*(+gen) concerning; (+acc) around*
περιπατέω	*I walk (about), live, behave*
Πέτρος, ου, ὁ	*Peter*
Πιλᾶτος, ου, ὁ	*Pilate*
πίνω	*I drink*
πίπτω	*I fall, collapse*
πιστεύω	*I believe, trust*
πίστις, εως, ἡ	*belief, faithfulness, trust, fidelity, faith*
πιστός, ή, όν	*faithful, trustworthy, believing*
πληρόω	*I fill, complete, fulfill*
πλοῖον, ου, τό	*boat, ship, vessel*
πνεῦμα, ατος, τό	*spirit, breath*
ποιέω	*I make, do*
πόλις, εως, ἡ	*town, city*
πολύς, πολλή, πολύ	*much, many*
πονηρός, ά, όν	*evil, bad, worthless, sick*
πορεύομαι	*I go, walk*
πούς, ποδός, ὁ	*foot*
πρεσβύτερος, α, ον	*aged, old;* (Subst.) *elder*
πρός	*(+acc) to, toward, with*
προσέρχομαι	*I go to, visit, approach*
προσεύχομαι	*I pray, petition a deity*
προσκυνέω	*I worship, prostrate myself*
πρόσωπον, ου, τό	*face, appearance, expression, presence*

προφήτης, ου, ὁ	*prophet*
πρῶτος, η, ον	*first, most prominent*
πῦρ, ός, τό	*fire*
πῶς	*how?*

Ρ ρ

ῥῆμα, ατος, τό	*word, saying, thing*

Σ σ

σάββατον, ου, τό	*Sabbath*
σάρξ, σαρκός, ἡ	*flesh, muscle, body*
σημεῖον, ου, τό	*sign, mark, signal, miracle*
Σίμων, ωνος, ὁ	*Simon*
σοφία, ας, ἡ	*wisdom, sound judgement*
σπείρω	*I sow seed, scatter*
στόμα, ατος, τό	*mouth, opening*
σύ, σοῦ; ὑμεῖς, ὑμῶν	*you; you all*
σύν	*(+dat) with, along with*
συνάγω	*I gather together, collect; receive as a guest*
συναγωγή, ῆς, ἡ	*assembly, gathering; synagogue*
σῴζω	*I save, rescue, keep safe*
σῶμα, ατος, τό	*body*

Τ τ

τέ	*and, so*
τέκνον, ου, τό	*child*
τηρέω	*I watch over, guard, keep*
τίθημι	*I put, place, lay*
τις, τι	*someone, something*
τίς, τί	*who? which? what?*
τοιοῦτος, αύτη, οῦτον	*such as this, of such a kind*

τόπος, ου, ὁ	*place, position*
τότε	*at that time, then*
τρεῖς, τρία	*three*
τρίτος, η, ον	*third*
τυφλός, ή, όν	*blind (often metaph.)*

Υ υ

ὕδωρ, ατος, τό	*water, rain*
υἱός, οῦ, ὁ	*son*
ὑπάγω	*I withdraw, go away*
ὑπάρχω	*I am present, at one's disposal; I am, exist*
ὑπέρ	*(+gen) on behalf of, for; (+acc) over, beyond*
ὑπό	*(+gen) by; (+acc) underneath*

Φ φ

Φαρισαῖος, ου, ὁ	*Pharisee, Separatist*
φέρω	*I carry, bring, lead*
φημί	*I say, declare*
φοβέω	*I fear, respect; I flee frightened*
φωνή, ῆς, ἡ	*voice, sound, communication*
φῶς, φωτός, τό	*light, torch*

Χ χ

χαίρω	*I am glad, rejoice, welcome*
χαρά, ᾶς, ἡ	*joy, delight, gladness*
χάρις, ιτος, ἡ	*grace, thankfulness, kindness*
χείρ, χειρός, ἡ	*hand*
Χριστός, οῦ, ὁ	*Messiah, Anointed One, Christ*
χρόνος, ου, ὁ	*time, occasion,*

Ψ ψ

ψυχή, ῆς, ἡ	*soul, life*

Ω ω

ὧδε	*here, thus, in this way, exceedingly so*
ὥρα, ας, ἡ	*hour, time, period, season*
ὡς	*as, like*
ὥστε	*so that, therefore, consequently*

Appendix IV

PARADIGMS

Athematic (μι) Stems: no connecting vowels

	Primary Tense				Secondary/Historical Tense			
	Active		Middle/Passive		Active		Middle/Passive	
	Singular	Plural	Singular	Plural	Singular	Plural	Singular	Plural
1st	μι	μεν	μαι	μεθα	ν	μεν	μην	μεθα
2nd	ς	τε	σαι	σθε	ς	τε	σο	σθε
3rd	σι(ν)	ασι(ν)	ται	νται	-	σαν	το	ντο

Thematic (ω) Stems: connecting vowel included

	Primary Tense				Secondary/Historical Tense			
	Active		Middle/Passive		Active		Middle/Passive	
	Singular	Plural	Singular	Plural	Singular	Plural	Singular	Plural
1st	ω	ομεν	ομαι	ομεθα	ον	ομεν	ομην	ομεθα
2nd	εις	ετε	ῃ	εσθε	ες	ετε	ου	εσθε
3rd	ει	ουσι	εται	ονται	- / ε	ον	ετο	οντο

Imperative (using λύω)

			Active	Middle	Passive
Present	Singular	2nd	λῦε	λύου	
		3rd	λυέτω	λυέσθω	
	Plural	2nd	λύετε	λύεσθε	
		3rd	λυέτωσαν	λυέσθωσαν	
Aorist	Singular	2nd	λῦσον	λῦσαι	λύθητι
		3rd	λυσάτω	λυσάσθω	λυθήτω
	Plural	2nd	λύσατε	λύσασθε	λύθητε
		3rd	λυσάτωσαν	λυσάσθωσαν	λυθήτωσαν

Infinitive (using λύω)

	Active	Middle	Passive
Present	λυείν	λύεσθαι	
Aorist	λῦσαι	λύσασθαι	λυθῆναι
Perfect	λελυκέναι	λελύσθαι	

Participle (using λύω)

			Present		Aorist			Perfect	
			Act.	Mid./Pass.	Act.	Mid.	Pass.	Act.	Mid./Pass.
Masculine	Singular	Nom.	λύων	λυόμενος	λύσας	λυσάμενος	λυθείς	λελυκώς	λελυμένος
		Gen.	λύοντος	λυομένου	λύσαντος	λυσαμένου	λυθέντος	λελυκότος	λελυμένου
		Dat.	λύοντι	λυομένῳ	λύσαντι	λυσαμένῳ	λυθέντι	λελυκότι	λελυμένῳ
		Acc.	λύοντα	λυόμενον	λύσαντα	λυσάμενον	λυθέντα	λελυκότα	λελυμένον
	Plural	Nom.	λύοντες	λυόμενοι	λύσαντες	λυσάμενοι	λυθέντες	λελυκότες	λελυμένοι
		Gen.	λυόντων	λυομένων	λυσάντων	λυσαμένων	λυθέντων	λελυκότων	λελυμένων
		Dat.	λύουσι(ν)	λυομένοις	λύσασι(ν)	λυσαμένοις	λυθεῖσι(ν)	λελυκόσι(ν)	λελυμένοις
		Acc.	λύοντας	λυομένους	λύσαντας	λυσαμένους	λυθέντας	λελυκότας	λελυμένους
Feminine	Singular	Nom.	λύουσα	λυομένη	λύσασα	λυσαμένη	λυθεῖσα	λελυκυῖα	λελυμένη
		Gen.	λυούσης	λυομένης	λυσάσης	λυσαμένης	λυθείσης	λελυκυίας	λελυμένης
		Dat.	λυούσῃ	λυομένῃ	λυσάσῃ	λυσαμένῃ	λυθείσῃ	λελυκυίᾳ	λελυμένῃ
		Acc.	λύουσαν	λυομένην	λύσασαν	λυσαμένην	λυθεῖσαν	λελυκυῖαν	λελυμένην
	Plural	Nom.	λύουσαι	λυόμεναι	λύσασαι	λυσάμεναι	λυθεῖσαι	λελυκυῖαι	λελυμέναι
		Gen.	λυουσῶν	λυομένων	λυσασῶν	λυσαμένων	λυθεισῶν	λελυκυιῶν	λελυμένων
		Dat.	λυούσαις	λυομέναις	λυσάσαις	λυσαμέναις	λυθείσαις	λελυκυίαις	λελυμέναις
		Acc.	λυούσας	λυομένας	λυσάσας	λυσαμένας	λυθείσας	λελυκυίας	λελυμένας
Neuter	Singular	Nom.	λῦον	λυόμενον	λῦσαν	λυσάμενον	λυθέν	λελυκός	λελυμένον
		Gen.	λύοντος	λυομένου	λύσαντος	λυσαμένου	λυθέντος	λελυκότος	λελυμένου
		Dat.	λύοντι	λυομένῳ	λύσαντι	λυσαμένῳ	λυθέντι	λελυκότι	λελυμένῳ
		Acc.	λῦον	λυόμενον	λῦσαν	λυσάμενον	λυθέν	λελυκός	λελυμένον
	Plural	Nom.	λύοντα	λυόμενα	λύσαντα	λυσάμενα	λυθέντα	λελυκότα	λελυμένα
		Gen.	λυόντων	λυομένων	λυσάντων	λυσαμένων	λυθέντων	λελυκότων	λελυμένων
		Dat.	λύουσι(ν)	λυομένοις	λύσασι(ν)	λυσαμένοις	λυθεῖσι(ν)	λελυκόσι(ν)	λελυμένοις
		Acc.	λύοντα	λυόμενα	λύσαντα	λυσάμενα	λυθέντα	λελυκότα	λελυμένα

Subjunctive

(Aor Act. add -σ-; Aor Pass. add -θ-)

	Active		Middle/Passive	
	Sing.	Plur.	Sing.	Plur.
1st	ω	ωμεν	ωμαι	ωμεθα
2nd	ῃς	ητε	ῃ	ησθε
3rd	ῃ	ωσι(ν)	ηται	ωνται

Optative

	Active		Middle/Passive	
	Sing.	Plur.	Sing.	Plur.
1st	μι / ν	μεν	μην	μεθα
2nd	ς	τε	σο	σθε
3rd	-	εν / σαν	το	ντο

Thematic Formation:
Pres: -οι + ending
Aor A/M: -σαιη + ending
Aor P: -θειη + ending

Athematic Formation:
Pres: -ιη or -ι + ending
Aor A/M/P: -ιη or -ι + ending

Present Indicative

	Sing.	Plur.
1st	εἰμί	ἐσμέν
2nd	εἶ	ἐστέ
3rd	ἐστί(ν)	εἰσί(ν)

Imperfect Indicative

	Sing.	Plur.
1st	ἤμην	ἦμεν
2nd	ἦς	ἦτε
3rd	ἦν	ἦσαν

Future Indicative

	Sing.	Plur.
1st	ἔσομαι	ἐσόμεθα
2nd	ἔσῃ	ἔσεσθε
3rd	ἔσται	ἔσονται

Present Subjunctive

	Sing.	Plur.
1st	ὦ	ὦμεν
2nd	ᾖς	ἦτε
3rd	ᾖ	ὦσι(ν)

Present Imperative

	Sing.	Plur.
2nd	ἴσθι	ἔστε
3rd	ἔστω	ἔστωσαν

Present Optative

	Sing.	Plur.
1st	εἴην	εἶμεν/εἴημεν
2nd	εἴης	εἶτε/εἴητε
3rd	εἴη	εἶεν/εἴησαν

Infinitive

Present	εἶναι
Future	ἔσεσθαι

Present Participle

		Masc.	Fem.	Neut.
Singular	Nom.	ὤν	οὖσα	ὄν
	Gen.	ὄντος	οὔσης	ὄντος
	Dat.	ὄντι	οὔσῃ	ὄντι
	Acc.	ὄντα	οὖσαν	ὄν
Plural	Nom.	ὄντες	οὖσαι	ὄντα
	Gen.	ὄντων	οὐσῶν	ὄντων
	Dat.	οὖσι(ν)	οὔσαις	οὖσι(ν)
	Acc.	ὄντας	οὔσας	ὄντα

Definite Article

	Singular			Plural		
	Masc.	Fem.	Neut.	Masc.	Fem.	Neut.
Nom.	ὁ	ἡ	τό	οἱ	αἱ	τά
Gen.	τοῦ	τῆς	τοῦ	τῶν		
Dat.	τῷ	τῇ	τῷ	τοῖς	ταῖς	τοῖς
Acc.	τόν	τήν	τό	τούς	τάς	τά

1st Declension Endings

	Singular				Plur.
	ε, ι, ρ	σ, ζ, ξ, ψ	all other	Masc.	
Nom.	α	α	η	ης	αι
Gen.	ας	ης	ης	ου	ων
Dat.	ᾳ	ῃ	ῃ	ῃ	αις
Acc.	αν	αν	ην	ην	ας

2nd Declension Endings

	Singular			Plural		
	Masc.	Fem.	Neut.	Masc.	Fem.	Neut.
Nom.	ος		ον	οι		α
Gen.	ου			ων		
Dat.	ῳ			οις		
Acc.	ον			ους		α

3rd Declension Endings

	Singular			Plural		
	Masc.	Fem.	Neut.	Masc.	Fem.	Neut.
Nom.	ς / -		-	ες		α
Gen.	ος			ων		
Dat.	ι			σι(ν)		
Acc.	α / ν		-	ας / ες		α

πᾶς, πᾶσα, πᾶν | 3-1-3

	Singular			Plural		
	Masc.	Fem.	Neut.	Masc.	Fem.	Neut.
Nom.	πᾶς	πᾶσα	πᾶν	πάντες	πᾶσαι	πάντα
Gen.	παντός	πάσης	παντός	πάντων	πασῶν	πάντων
Dat.	παντί	πάσῃ	παντί	πᾶσι(ν)	πάσαις	πᾶσι(ν)
Acc.	πάντα	πᾶσαν	πᾶν	πάντας	πάσας	πάντα

πολύς, πολλή, πολύ | 2-1-2

	Singular			Plural		
	Masc.	Fem.	Neut.	Masc.	Fem.	Neut.
Nom.	πολύς	πολλή	πολύ	πολλοί	πολλαί	πολλά
Gen.	πολλοῦ	πολλῆς	πολλοῦ	πολλῶν		
Dat.	πολλῷ	πολλῇ	πολλῷ	πολλοῖς	πολλαῖς	πολλοῖς
Acc.	πολύν	πολλήν	πολύ	πολλούς	πολλάς	πολλά

Personal Pronouns: *I, we, you, she, he, it, they*

	1st		2nd	
	Sing.	Plur.	Sing.	Plur.
Nom.	ἐγώ	ἡμεῖς	σύ	ὑμεῖς
Gen.	(ἐ)μοῦ	ἡμῶν	σοῦ	ὑμῶν
Dat.	(ἐ)μοί	ἡμῖν	σοί	ὑμῖν
Acc.	(ἐ)μέ	ἡμᾶς	σέ	ὑμᾶς

	3rd					
	Singular			Plural		
	Masc.	Fem.	Neut.	Masc.	Fem.	Neut.
Nom.	αὐτός	αὐτή	αὐτό	αὐτοί	αὐταί	αὐτά
Gen.	αὐτοῦ	αὐτῆς	αὐτοῦ	αὐτῶν		
Dat.	αὐτῷ	αὐτῇ	αὐτῷ	αὐτοῖς	αὐταῖς	αὐτοῖς
Acc.	αὐτόν	αὐτήν	αὐτό	αὐτούς	αὐτάς	αὐτά

Proximal (Near) Demonstrative: *this, these*

	Singular			Plural		
	Masc.	Fem.	Neut.	Masc.	Fem.	Neut.
Nom.	οὗτος	αὕτη	τοῦτο	οὗτοι	αὗται	ταῦτα
Gen.	τούτου	ταύτης	τούτου	τούτων		
Dat.	τούτῳ	ταύτῃ	τούτῳ	τούτοις	ταύταις	τούτοις
Acc.	τοῦτον	ταύτην	τοῦτο	τούτους	ταύτας	ταῦτα

Distal (Far) Demonstrative: *that, those*

	Singular			Plural		
	Masc.	Fem.	Neut.	Masc.	Fem.	Neut.
Nom.	ἐκεῖνος	ἐκείνη	ἐκεῖνο	ἐκεῖνοι	ἐκεῖναι	ἐκεῖνα
Gen.	ἐκείνου	ἐκείνης	ἐκείνου	ἐκείνων		
Dat.	ἐκείνῳ	ἐκείνῃ	ἐκείνῳ	ἐκείνοις	ἐκείναις	ἐκείνοις
Acc.	ἐκεῖνον	ἐκεῖνην	ἐκεῖνο	ἐκείνους	ἐκείνας	ἐκεῖνα

Interrogative Pronouns: *who? which? what?*

	Singular			Plural		
	Masc.	Fem.	Neut.	Masc.	Fem.	Neut.
Nom.	τίς		τί	τίνες		τίνα
Gen.	τίνος			τίνων		
Dat.	τίνι			τίσι(ν)		
Acc.	τίνα		τί	τίνας		τίνα

Indefinite Pronouns: *someone, something*

	Singular			Plural		
	Masc.	Fem.	Neut.	Masc.	Fem.	Neut.
Nom.	τις		τι	τινες		τινα
Gen.	τινος			τινων		
Dat.	τινι			τισι(ν)		
Acc.	τινα		τι	τινας		τινα

Indefinite Relative Pronouns: *whoever, whichever, every one who*

	Singular			Plural		
	Masc.	Fem.	Neut.	Masc.	Fem.	Neut.
Nom.	ὅστις	ἥτις	ὅ τι / ὅτι	οἵτινες	αἵτινες	ἅτινα
Gen.	οὗτινος	ἧστινος	οὗτινος		ὧντινων	
Dat.	ᾧτινι	ᾗτινι	ᾧτινι	οἷστισι(ν)	αἷστισι(ν)	οἷστισι(ν)
Acc.	ὅντινα	ἥντινα	ὅ τι / ὅτι	οὕστινας	ἅστινας	ἅτινα

Relative Pronouns: *who, which, that*

	Singular			Plural		
	M	F	N	M	F	N
Nom.	ὅς	ἥ	ὅ	οἵ	αἵ	ἅ
Gen.	οὗ	ἧς	οὗ		ὧν	
Dat.	ᾧ	ᾗ	ᾧ	οἷς	αἷς	οἷς
Acc.	ὅν	ἥν	ὅ	οὕς	ἅς	ἅ

Reciprocal Pronouns: *one another*

	Plural
Gen.	ἀλλήλων
Dat.	ἀλλήλοις
Acc.	ἀλλήλους

Reflexive Pronouns: *myself, yourself, herself, himself, itself*

		1st		2nd		3rd		
		Masc.	Fem.	Masc.	Fem.	Masc.	Fem.	Neut.
Singular	Gen.	ἐμαυτοῦ	ἐμαυτῆς	σεαυτοῦ	σεαυτῆς	ἑαυτοῦ	ἑαυτῆς	ἑαυτοῦ
	Dat.	ἐμαυτῷ	ἐμαυτῇ	σεαυτῷ	σεαυτῇ	ἑαυτῷ	ἑαυτῇ	ἑαυτῷ
	Acc.	ἐμαυτόν	ἐμαυτήν	σεαυτόν	σεαυτήν	ἑαυτόν	ἑαυτήν	ἑαυτό
Plural	Gen.	ἑαυτῶν		ἑαυτῶν		ἑαυτῶν		
	Dat.	ἑαυτοῖς	ἑαυταῖς	ἑαυτοῖς	ἑαυταῖς	ἑαυτοῖς	ἑαυταῖς	ἑαυτοῖς
	Acc.	ἑαυτούς	ἑαυτάς	ἑαυτούς	ἑαυτάς	ἑαυτούς	ἑαυτάς	ἑαυτά

www.ingramcontent.com/pod-product-compliance
Lightning Source LLC
Chambersburg PA
CBHW070045100426
42740CB00013B/2813

9781942697879